WHY SHOULD I GO TO VALENCIA

WHY SHOULD I GO TO ↓
VALENCIA

THE CITY YOU DEFINITELY NEED TO
VISIT BEFORE YOU TURN 30 (OR 130)

(m)

THIS IS WHY!

Valencia offers an exciting mix of history, modern vibes, beaches, and green spaces. Whether you're into art, food, sports, or festivals, Valencia has everything to make your trip unforgettable.

A must-visit is the futuristic City of Arts and Sciences. The gigantic white structures look like they came from another planet. Take Insta-worthy pics, walk through Europe's largest aquarium, and catch a film at the IMAX cinema. Then head to the historic centre and explore the cathedral, climb the Torres de Serranos for stunning views, and wander the streets of El Carmen, filled with street art, vintage shops, and hidden bars.

Valencia is also foodie paradise. It is the home of paella, so enjoy one at Malvarrosa Beach or hit a tapas bar in the Cabanyal neighbourhood. And don't forget to try *horchata* (a sweet local drink made from tiger nuts).

Outdoor lovers will feel at home too. Named Green Capital of Europe in 2024, Valencia offers the Jardín del Turía for relaxing and the nearby Albufera Natural Park for bird watching, boat rides, and stunning sunsets. You can also hike the nearby mountains and take in the natural beauty.

With its student life, sunny beaches, and nightlife lasting until dawn, Valencia is the ultimate spot to make memories, meet new people, and experience a city that is as fun as it is beautiful.

CONTENTS

DISTRICTS 8
PRACTICAL INFO 12

FOOD AND DRINKS 104
GOING OUT 126

WHEN TO TRAVEL 28
LIFE IN VALENCIA 38

SHOPPING 140

GREEN VALENCIA 170
OUTSIDE OF VALENCIA 184

Index 188
Who made this book? 191-192

DISTRICTS

Ciutat Vella

The old town, Ciutat Vella, is a lively district known for its medieval charm and narrow streets. Iconic landmarks include the Cathedral, La Lonja de la Seda (The Silk Exchange), and the bustling Central Market. Its *plazas*, museums, and mix of Gothic, Baroque, and modern architecture reflect the city's rich history.

La Saïdia

The district La Saïdia is named after Zayd Abu Zayd (the last Almohad governor of Valencia) and blends tradition with urban life. It features charming neighbourhoods, such as Morvedre and Marxalenes, and landmarks like the 14th-century

Serranos Towers. Known for its parks, cultural heritage, and proximity to the old Turia riverbed, it's a lively area with deep local character.

L'Eixample

The elegant L'Eixample is a centrally located district, known for its wide avenues, modernist architecture, and vibrant nightlife. Featuring upscale shopping, dining, and bars, it includes neighbourhoods like Ruzafa, famous for its artsy vibe and markets. Its tree-lined streets and cultural venues make it a sought-after urban hub.

Extramurs

The diverse district Extramurs (meaning 'beyond the walls') borders the historic centre. It's known for cultural sites like the Botanical Garden and Torres de Quart. With a mix of residential and commercial spaces, it offers a blend of tradition and modernity.

El Pla del Real

The elegant area El Pla del Real is known for its spacious boulevards, parks, and cultural landmarks. Home to the University of Valencia, it includes iconic spots like the Mestalla Stadium and Monforte Gardens. It is a mix of residential calm and urban accessibility.

Benimaclet

Once a village, Benimaclet is now a vibrant, bohemian area. Known for its community spirit, it blends traditional charm with a youthful, multicultural vibe. Its lively streets feature local markets, bars, and cultural spaces. Popular with students and artists, Benimaclet thrives on creativity, festivals, and a welcoming atmosphere.

Quatre Carreres

Quatre Carreres blends tradition and modernity. It houses the futuristic City of Arts and Sciences and the Roig Arena, making it a cultural hotspot. Known for its residential areas and sports facilities, it attracts families and visitors to its evolving urban landscape.

Camins al Grau

The district Camins al Grau bridges the city centre and the beach. Known for its modern vibe, it features residential areas, local markets, and commercial hubs. Close to the City of Arts and Sciences, it offers a dynamic mix of urban living and cultural accessibility.

Algiros

The youthful energy of Algiros is driven by its proximity to universities. It features a mix of student-friendly amenities, local markets, and parks like Ayora Gardens. With diverse dining options and excellent transport links, Algiros offers a multicultural atmosphere and an urban lifestyle.

Poblats Maritims

The coastal district Poblats Marítims includes picturesque neighbourhoods like Cabanyal and Malvarrosa. Known for its colourful houses, historic fishing roots, and lively beaches, it offers a mix of tradition and modernity. A must-visit for the seafood restaurants, traditions like Semana Santa Marinera, and its overall maritime charm.

TRAVEL

When arriving at the airport, you can take a taxi directly outside the arrival hall. The price to or from the airport is €25-30. Bus 150 takes forty minutes to reach the city centre and departs every thirty minutes. You can buy a single ticket on the bus for €4.80. But the most common means of transportation from the airport is the metro. Follow the signs at the airport; metro 3 and 5 leave every ten to fifteen minutes. A single ticket costs €4.80, or you can purchase a TuiN card when you first arrive.

If you arrive at either Estacion del Norte or Estacion Sorolla (for high-speed trains), you will already be in central Valencia and will find plenty of public transport connections from there.

You might want to think ahead about how you plan to get around Valencia. If not, you'll end up walking 30,000+ steps a day. The distance between the beach and the city centre is around 6 kilometres and the Jardín del Turía spreads over about 10 kilometres. Cycling is a much easier way to cover the distance. There are over 200 kilometres of bike lanes, which is extraordinary for Spain. You can rent a bike on just about any street corner. Examples include Passionbike, The Easy Way, The Happy Tourist, Valencia Bikes, and Virgin Bikes. Another option is Valenbisi, the bike-sharing programme. Their bikes are parked in one of the 276 parking spots across the city centre. Short-term rental is €3.90 per day or €13.30 for a week. The first half an hour is free, the first hour after costs €1.04, and after

that you'll be charged €3.12 an hour. Access is easy, the price is right, but their bikes are not as comfortable as regular city bikes.

The bus is a good option in Valencia, as many bus lines cover the city, and you can reach any address quickly. It works best to use Google Maps, Moovit or the EMT Valencia app to find your way around. The nearest bus stop and number will be indicated, as well as the journey time. Buy a single ticket for €1.50 on the bus using card or cash or buy a Bonobús 10 pass at one of the kiosks or *tabacos* around town (look for the bus company EMT's sticker).

Metro Valencia has ten metro lines, and these connect the city centre to the airport, the beach and the outskirts. It is a fast way to travel. Tickets can be bought at metro station counters or machines. A single ticket within the city costs €1.50 or you can buy a SUMA 10 (with ten bus, tram, or metro fares) for €8. For the reusable card itself you pay €2 initial costs, and it can be used by multiple people. If you know that you are going to use the metro and tram a lot, a TuiN card gives better value for money. The card registers the distance you cover, and charges 50% less than a single ticket. It can also be used for trips to and from the airport.

Any white taxi displaying a green light can be hailed. Cabify and Freenow are the most commonly used taxi apps. In the city centre, a trip costs around €8-10. You can pay by cash or card.

You can rent a scooter to cross the city at Cooltra, RideOn or Yego, to name a few examples. Or try an e-scooter at one of the bike shops. In Valencia, e-scooters are allowed on bike lanes. A helmet is mandatory, and the minimal age is 16 years.

WHERE TO STAY

Red & Purple Nest Hostel

Carrer de la Pau 36, 46003 Ciutat Vella; Plaça de Tetuan 5, 46003 Ciutat Vella, nesthostelsvalencia.com

The Red & Purple Nest hostels are located near each other in the historic city centre. Both the private rooms and dormitories are bright, colourful, and spacious. However, the standout features are the communal areas and the numerous activities that take place.

Home Youth Hostel Valencia

Carrer de la Llotja 4, 46001 Ciutat Vella, homeyouthhostel.com

Valencia's first hostel without bunk beds. Home Youth Hostel is ideal for both groups and solo travellers, and provides centrally located, budget-friendly accommodation. The rooms are vibrant and uniquely designed with original wall art.

The River Hostel

Plaça del Temple 6, 46003 Ciutat Vella, riverhostelvalencia.com

The views over Jardín del Turia are the best from the private or shared rooms of The River Hostel. The shared rooms are for 4, 6, 8, 10 or 12, and there is a girls-only room. The small restaurant by the reception area serves a fantastic breakfast and occasionally makes paella. Ask for their famous pub quiz, bar crawl or bike rental.

Capsule Inn

Carrer de Sant Vicent Màrtir 144, 46007 Extramurs, capsuleinnvalencia.com

For those who aren't claustrophobic, the capsule dormitories of Capsule Inn offer an affordable way to stay in Valencia. With neon lights and space-themed decor, the place resembles the interior of Star Wars' Millennium Falcon.

Casual Valencia Vintage

casualhoteles.com

Hotels with themed rooms in various locations close to the city's top attractions. Casual Valencia Vintage's themes include vintage styles, music from the 70s, 80s, and 90s, classic films, and Valencian traditions. These budget-friendly hotels are fun, relaxed, and full of character.

Mythic Valencia

Carrer del Poeta Monmeneu 16, 46009 La Saïdia, mythichotel.es

On entering the B&B Mythic Valencia, you'll still see traces of its former life as an industrial warehouse. Each comfortable room features a unique interior design, and the urban art walls leave a striking impression on all visitors. Breakfast is included with your stay.

Up Hostel

Carrer de Xàtiva 24, 46007 Extramurs, valenciauphostel.com

Inside the bustling central railway station, you'll find a tranquil oasis to sleep and relax in, Up Hostel. You can meet people and enjoy drinks or meals at the Go Bar. You'll also be close to all major attractions and have easy access to metro, train, and bus.

Nap V

Carrer de Finlàndia 14 Bajo, 46010 El Pla del Real, napvalencia.com

The minimalist and tranquil rooms of Nap V are ideal for unwinding after a busy day and night in the city. The staff is friendly, the communal areas are lovely, and lockers are available. Situated in a popular student district, the location is close to numerous student eateries, bars, and pubs.

Cantagua Youth Hostel

Carrer de Vicente Lleó 28, 46004 Quatre Carreres, cantaguahostel.com

You instantly feel at home when you enter Cantagua Youth Hostel. The warm, relaxed, and cheerful atmosphere welcomes those who appreciate life, art, and culture. It's not just a spot for a night's stay, but a gem to visit when you're in Valencia.

DWO Hotels

Avinguda del Port 129, 46022 Camins al Grau, dwohotels.com

This former wheat flour factory houses DWO Hotels with 126 luxurious yet affordable rooms. Key features include a garden with palm trees, parking facilities (including bicycle parking), beautifully renovated rooms, and a restaurant.

Bird House

Avinguda del Port 47, 46021 Camins al Grau, birdhouse.es

This bright and atmospheric hostel has original colourful tile floors and modern industrial accents. Bird House offers rooms for 2, 3, or 4 people, with shared or private bathrooms. The inviting communal spaces contribute to a homely atmosphere, making it a comfortable place to stay.

Urban Youth Hostel

Avinguda del Port 280, 46024 Poblats Marítims, urbanyouthhostel.com

You will find this vibrant youth hostel conveniently located near the beach. The Youth Bar is a fantastic spot to socialise or watch a match, while the spacious living area is perfect for reading a book. Every now and then, they organise salsa dance classes and out-of-town excursions.

GOOD TO KNOW

Opening Hours

Shops are typically open Mondays to Saturdays, from 10am to 2pm and from 5pm to 8pm. Department stores have longer hours, operating from 10am to 10pm continuously. During the Christmas season and sales periods, many shops also open on Sundays and holidays. Museums, monuments, and churches have varying opening hours. Generally, they open in the morning around 10am, close for lunch and a siesta at 2pm, and then reopen in the afternoon from 4pm till 8pm. Most museums are closed on Mondays but open on Sunday mornings, usually free of charge. Some museums, like the Bellas Artes and Centro del Carmen, are free, while others, such as the Science Museum in the City of Arts and Sciences, charge an entry fee.

Celebrations

Valencia is famous for its wide range of celebrations and traditions throughout the year. Many of the activities take place in the streets and include paella cooking, music, dance, processions, and fireworks. Notable celebrations in Valencia are Las Fallas in March, Corpus Christi in June, and Día de la Comunidad Valenciana on 9th October.

Eating habits

The Valencian community is known for its high density of bars and restaurants, with one restaurant for every 430 residents and one bar for every 148. Eating out is common practice and if you look in the right places, reasonably priced. The day begins with *desayuno*, a simple breakfast typically consisting of coffee with a croissant or toast topped with tomatoes, olive oil, and salt. The second meal, *almuerzo*, is an early lunch around 11am or noon, often featuring a sandwich with toppings like fried eggs or bacon. The main meal of the day, *comida*, is served at 1.30pm and usually consists of a hot dish. Many restaurants offer an affordable *menu del día* for lunch. At 5pm, bars serve tapas or a sweet snack for *merienda*. Dinner, or *la cena*, is a lighter meal served from 8pm – or later.

Tapas

The verb *tapar* describes a style of eating and sharing meals. It's typical to share your dishes. Start by ordering some dishes *para compartir* (to share), like *patatas bravas* (potatoes with a spicy and garlic sauce), *jamon* (cured ham) or a tomato salad with tasty Valencian tomatoes, and then choose a main dish, either fish or meat, to share as well. If you're uncertain about portion sizes, begin with one or two dishes per person. Check with the waiter, and order more if you still feel hungry.

Paella Valenciana & Horchata

Paella, originally from Valencia, is a traditional dish made with chicken, rabbit, butter beans, green beans, and saffron, cooked in chicken broth. In restaurants, you can also order a fish paella, or a vegetarian one. Valencians generally do not mix fish and meat in the same dish, as the emphasis is on the flavour of the broth. Only specialised paella restaurants serve a variety, and of course they have the best paellas. Other restaurants might make one big paella in advance and serve a portion for their lunch menu. Paella as a lunch dish is often enjoyed with family on weekends. The size of the pan

depends on the number of people participating. The rice should be cooked *al dente*, with a flavourful, crispy layer called *socarrat* at the bottom of the pan.

Horchata de chufa is a non-alcoholic beverage made from *chufa* (tiger nuts), sugar, and water. It is best enjoyed ice-cold, and is often accompanied by a pastry called *Farton*, which is dipped into the drink. Horchata is rich in minerals like magnesium, phosphorus, calcium, and iron, as well as vitamins C and E. With an energy value of 100 kcal per 100 g, it makes for an excellent energy drink and contains only a small amount of sodium.

Language

Spanish (Castellano) is the official language, though many street signs are also in Valenciano. It is considered a dialect of Catalan rather than Spanish. While it is not an official language, it is taught in schools alongside English. Most Valencians are willing to assist with directions or recommendations, even if their English is not perfect. If you don't speak Spanish, but French, you might be surprised how many Valencians understand you.

Weather

Valencia enjoys a Mediterranean climate with warm summers and mild winters, free from frost or snow. Summers and winters are mostly dry, but expect occasional heavy rain showers in September, October, March, and April. As the local saying goes, *'plou poc pero per a lo poc que plou, plou prou'* – it rains little, but when it does, it's enough. During the summer, it is advisable to stay out of the sun between 1pm and 5pm. To stay cool, consider shopping in air-conditioned shops or visiting museums.

Money and tipping

The currency in Valencia is the euro. Most restaurants and shops accept both cash and cards, but it is good to have some cash on hand. Tipping is not mandatory but leaving a few euros for good service is appreciated.

Safety

Valencia is a safe city and even at nighttime it is still busy outside. Police are always visibly present on the streets and helpful for directions or other questions concerning the city. But be careful of pickpockets. They typically look for vulnerable tourists at busy tourist spots, in the Jardín del Turía, and on public transport.

Dress code

When temperatures rise and beaches are full, some tourists might confuse the city's streets for a sunny beach and walk in the city centre shirtless. This is frowned upon by locals, and the police may tell you to put on a top.

VALENCIA IN SPRING

Spring in Valencia is filled with activities and celebrations. The most significant festival is Las Fallas, which takes place in March. The festivities begin on the last Sunday of February with a traditional opening ceremony. Daily firework displays run from 1st to 19th March, starting *mascletà* (firecrackers) at 2pm and culminating in midnight fireworks during the final five days. On 17th and 18th March, girls dressed in traditional attire (*falleras*) present flowers to Saint Mary at the Plaza de la Virgen. Statues are erected on the streets and can be visited before they are burnt on the final day of the festival, 19th March. The festival also features street music, paella cooking, and mobile dance parties.

In addition to Las Fallas, you might encounter other festivities such as Semana Santa Marinera, Virgen de los Desamparados, Corpus Christi, or other events like kite, book, wine, and food festivals, or a 15K night run. Almost every weekend, you'll find events happening in Jardín del Turía, the Port of Valencia, or the city's streets.

March also marks the bloom of orange trees, filling the air with the sweet scent of the white blossoms, called Azahar in Arabic — after which the name of Valencia's coastline, Costa Azahar, is named.

Spring temperatures start off cool but gradually warm as the days progress. April can be unpredictable, with occasional rain showers that may be heavy but are usually short-lived. The showers can start as early as March or extend into May.

VALENCIA IN SUMMER

Summer in Valencia brings rising temperatures and high humidity. A cooling sea breeze, known as the Levante wind, provides some relief. It's the perfect season to enjoy festivals, long beach days, siestas in the park, and socialising with friends.

In July, the city hosts the Feria de Julio, a summer festival featuring concerts in Viveros Park, street theatre, the Batalla de Flores ('flower battle'), and numerous other activities across town. Despite the heat, locals usually stay in the city to enjoy these summer celebrations. Come August, they leave the city for their holidays and some restaurants and shops may close. But fear not. Valencia has become a popular summer destination for both Spanish and foreign young people, so most bars and clubs remain open.

You can also visit the open-air cinemas, set in beautiful locations.

By early September, life in Valencia returns to normal. Everything reopens and smaller towns and neighbourhoods celebrate their own traditions. One of the most famous events is La Tomatina in Buñol, and on the last Wednesday of August, people from all over the world gather to throw tomatoes at each other.

Pro tip: If you want some shelter from the sun, you can stay cool in one of the large shopping centres around town. The *Rebajas* (sales) begin on 1st July. Alternatively, escape the heat by visiting one of the air-conditioned (and free) museums, like Bellas Artes.

VALENCIA IN AUTUMN

As summer comes to an end, the city returns to its regular rhythm of work and school, along with a variety of celebrations. A significant public holiday in the region is Día de la Comunidad Valenciana on 9th October. This festive day kicks off with fireworks, traditional attire, street music, and concludes with a colourful procession and more fireworks. 12th October marks the National Day of Spain, another bank holiday. November 1st is also a public holiday. Museums and art galleries launch new exhibitions following their summer breaks, ushering in new energy as the weather cools.

During autumn, temperatures remain relatively high. However, the phenomenon known as *la gota fría*, or *DANA*, can occur, bringing heavy rain, hailstorms, and thunderstorms that may last from a few hours to several days. While temperatures may drop, most days still remain sunny and warm, creating a mix where one day calls for a raincoat and a jumper, while the next may require shorts and a T-shirt.

Autumn is also the season for harvesting rice and grapes. Albufera is an excellent place to visit if you want to see the rice harvest. This time of year also attracts many bird species that come to feast on the harvest. It's the ideal time to enjoy paella in El Palmar, next to the rice fields. For grape harvesting, head to Utiel and Requena, where many wineries will start with their winemaking.

VALENCIA IN WINTER

In winter, temperatures can vary a lot from day to night. While nighttime temperatures may drop near freezing, daytime temperatures can go up to 20 degrees in sunny, sheltered spots. You will probably need your sunglasses and sunscreen — yes, even in winter. Rain is quite rare during this season. Winter is about the orange harvest season and enjoying freshly pressed orange juice.

The most significant events are Christmas Eve and New Year's Eve. Be sure to secure tickets for one of the great parties around town so you won't have to search open venues on the night. On New Year's Eve, it's tradition to eat one grape every second leading up to midnight, amounting to twelve grapes for good luck.

Christmas Day and New Year's Day are typically spent with family, with people either staying in or going out for lunch with relatives. At the end of the year, many participate in the San Silvestre 5K Run, and if you plan to join, consider wearing a festive costume.

You can also enjoy various holiday activities, such as Christmas shopping at numerous markets, ice skating, visiting nativity scenes (*Belens*), or strolling through the city at night to admire the Christmas lights and decorations.

On 6th January, Epiphany or Three Kings Day is celebrated. On this day, children receive gifts from one of the three wise men. The following day marks the start of the winter sales, *las rebajas*, and signifies the end of the Christmas season.

HISTORY

Valentia: Roman times

The city of Valencia was founded by the Romans in 138 BCE, located next to the Turia River, approximately 6 kilometres from the sea. This position offered fertile land and was easy to defend. The Romans improved the surrounding area by constructing aqueducts to transport water to drier regions. The central area, known as the Forum Romanum, is where the archaeological museum L'Almoina stands today. This site holds the largest number of remains from that period in Valencia. Nearby was the Roman Circus, a hippodrome. The circus, measuring 70 by 350 metres (roughly four football pitches), hosted races featuring twelve chariots divided into four teams, accommodating up to 10,000 spectators. The Romans referred to the city as Valentia, signifying 'bravery' or 'courage'. The horn of plenty (cornucopia) was the Roman symbol for Valentia and can still be seen at Plaza de la Virgen.

Costa Azahar

Each stretch of the Spanish coastline has its own name, and you might have heard of Costa Brava, Costa Blanca, and Costa del Sol. The coastline of Valencia is known as Costa Azahar, named after the Arabic name for orange blossom. During the Middle Ages, Valencia experienced an Islamic period from the 8th to the 13th century. Although many buildings from that time have been lost, the Arabs contributed significantly to the region in ways that are still relevant today. The Spanish language includes many words of Arabic origin, such as *azúcar* (sugar), *naranja* (orange), *arroz* (rice), *sandía* (watermelon), *aceite* (oil), and *albahaca* (basil). Oranges, rice, and palm trees, now commonly associated with Valencia and Spain, were all introduced by the Arabs, still commonly referred to as Moors in Spain. The irrigation system we know today was initiated by the Moors, featuring eight major canals that carry water from the mountains and the Turia River to farmers' fields, even during dry periods. The renowned Valencian water tribunal also dates back this era, where farmers resolved difficulties related to water management.

9th October

On 9th October, Valencia celebrates the *Día de la Comunidad Valenciana*, the regional day of Valencia, which also doubles as a local version of Valentine's Day called *San Donis*. On this day, lovers traditionally exchange silk scarves and marzipan shaped like fruits and vegetables. However, the day holds even greater historical significance. It commemorates the year 1238, when the Christian King Jaime I of Aragon conquered the city of Valencia from the Moors. Many legends stem from this event. According to one tale, Jaime I entered the city from the north on a hot day, riding his horse and feeling parched. A farmer's wife offered him a local drink, which the king instantly loved. He is said to have exclaimed, 'Es oro, xata', meaning 'It's gold, darling'. The beverage has since been called *orxata* in Valencian, or *horchata* in Spanish. Following the conquest, Jaime I expanded his empire further south. The Crown of Aragon, at its peak, included Catalonia, Valencia, the Balearic Islands, Sardinia, southern Italy, and even parts of Greece. This shared history has resulted in lasting cultural,

celebratory, and linguistic similarities across these regions.

The Silk Road

The Silk Road, originating from Eastern Asia, including China, served as a major trade route that transported silk and other goods to European countries. During the 15th century, Valencia became a wealthy city and an important port along this route and profited greatly from the silk trade. Soon after, Valencian farmers learnt about the silkworms that fed on the leaves of mulberry trees and their cocoons, and many farmers began to profit from silk production as well. At the Silk Museum, Museo de la Seda, visitors can learn about the process of silk production, its use in fashion, and other aspects of the luxurious lifestyle of that period. The Silk Exchange, Lonja de la Seda, was constructed between 1482 and 1548 and stands as one of Valencia's most important landmarks. The main trading hall, Sala de Contratación, was completed within the first fifteen years of construction. Since 1996, this masterpiece of late Gothic architecture has been recognised as a UNESCO World Heritage site, representing the Mediterranean's wealth at the time.

Parque Glorieta

During the First French Empire, Valencia proved to be a challenging city for the French to conquer. In June 1808, after several failed attempts, Napoleon's Marshal Moncey was defeated in the Battle of Valencia during the Peninsular War, forcing the French to retreat to Madrid. Evidence of the fierce battles remains visible today in the Torres de Quart, where cannonball marks from the French assault can still be seen. It wasn't until 1811 that the French completed the Siege of Valencia. During this time, Joseph Bonaparte, Napoleon's elder brother and pretender to the Spanish throne, moved the royal court to Valencia, where it remained until the French were defeated at the Battle of Vitoria in June 1813. During this brief period of French control, the city's first public park, Parque Glorieta, was established within the city walls and it features monumental ficus trees today.

Valencian Art Nouveau

Catalan Modernism was a cultural and artistic movement that originated in Catalonia. Some key figures in the development of Modernist architecture in the late 19th and early 20th centuries were the architects Lluís Domènech i Montaner, Josep Puig i Cadafalch, and Antoni Gaudí. Their bold, colourful designs, featuring ceramics, stained glass, cast iron, and organic forms, inspired many Valencian architects, leading to a regional style known as Modernismo Valenciano, or Valencian Art Nouveau. One of the most notable examples is the Mercado de Colón, built by Francisco Mora Berenguer between 1914 and 1916. Another landmark is the Estación del Norte, completed in 1917 by Demetrio Ribes in collaboration with the company Caminos de Hierro del Norte de España. The third significant building from this era is the Mercado Central, designed by Francesc Guàrdia i Vial and Alexandre Soler i March in 1914, though it did not open until 1928. While these are the most famous examples in Valencia, Valencian Art Nouveau can be seen throughout the city.

Capital of the Republic

During the Spanish Civil War (1936-1939), Valencia temporarily became the capital of the Spanish Republic after the Republican government moved from Madrid. Valencia remained the capital until October 1937, when the government relocated to Barcelona. However, the city continued to be a crucial Republican stronghold throughout 1938, even as Nationalist forces steadily advanced. Valencia endured severe air raids during the war, with Italian and German planes supporting Franco's Nationalists, repeatedly bombing the city. These bombings targeted civilian areas to weaken morale and hasten Republican collapse. To protect residents from the frequent air raids, bomb shelters were constructed across the city. One of the best-known is Refugio del Ayuntamiento, located beneath the town hall, which served as a safe haven for civilians during the attacks. Despite these defensive measures, Valencia's strategic position weakened. On 30th March 1939, Franco's forces entered the city, marking the fall of one of the last Republican strongholds. Just days later, the Spanish Civil War officially ended with the Nationalists' victory, leading to the establishment of Franco's dictatorship.

Contemporary identity

Three renowned architects made significant contributions at the turn of the 21st century. Santiago Calatrava, a native of Valencia, designed the City of Arts and Sciences, a futuristic complex featuring cultural and scientific buildings with bold, organic forms. David Chipperfield created Veles e Vents, a minimalist structure at the Valencia marina for the 2007 America's Cup, known for its open terraces and sleek design. Norman Foster designed the Valencia Congress Centre, a modern, sustainable venue completed in 1998, recognised for its glass façade and wave-like roof. These architects have played a pivotal role in Valencia's transformation into a hub of modern, world-class architecture. Calatrava's futuristic designs, Chipperfield's minimalism, and Foster's high-tech, sustainable structures are now key elements of the city's identity.

↓ TORRES DE QUART

SIGHTSEEING

Basilica de Mare de Déu

Plaça de la Verge, 46001 Ciutat Vella, basilicadesamparados.org

The Basilica de la Mare de Déu, a small Catholic church built in the 17th century in Baroque style, is located on Plaza de la Virgen. Its name, meaning 'Mother of God', and the square's name, 'Virgin Square', highlight the region's deep devotion to Saint Mary. Inside the church, a statue of Mary is prominently displayed above the altar. The basilica is always bustling with activity, hosting seven to eight masses a day. During special occasions and in May, the statue is carried in a procession through the city and surrounding villages, as part of local religious celebrations.

Torres de Serranos

Plaça dels Furs, 46003 Ciutat Vella

Torres de Serranos is part of Valencia's medieval defensive works built in the 14th century. Originally, there were twelve gates connected by city walls. Now only two remain: Torres de Serranos and Torres de Quart, with a small section of the original wall still standing near Torres de Quart. The gates, which also served as watchtowers, are 33 metres high. Before the city walls were demolished in 1865 to allow for urban expansion, the two gates were in use as prisons for wealthy inmates, which is why they were preserved. You can climb both gates on certain days for free, including Sundays and holidays. On other days, you will be charged a small fee.

City of Arts and Sciences

Avinguda del Professor López Piñero 1, 46013 Quatre Carreres, cac.es

The City of Arts and Sciences was designed by Valencian architect Santiago Calatrava, with construction spanning from the project's start in 1989 to its completion in 2009, with the final building the Àgora (now the CaixaForum). The first structure completed was L'Hemisfèric, an IMAX cinema, in 1998, often referred to as 'the eye' due to its shape. Two years later, the Science Museum opened, followed by L'Oceanogràfic aquarium and the Palau de les Arts opera house. While most buildings can be explored freely, entry to exhibitions, performances, and certain areas requires a ticket.

Estación del Norte

Carrer de Bailèn 34, 46007 L'Eixample

Despite being located in the southern part of the city, Valencia's main train station is called Estación del Norte. Its name is derived from a steel company from the north of Spain, Compañía de Hierro del Norte de España. Similar stations once existed in Barcelona and Madrid, but they were later renamed. Built in 1917, Estación del Norte serves short and medium-distance trains . Notable features include the original wooden ticket desks, a former waiting room with tiled walls, Art Nouveau lamps, and mosaic panels that display the words 'pleasant journey' in various languages, reflecting its rich history and design.

Ayuntamiento

Plaça de l'Ajuntament 1, 46002 Ciutat Vella

The early 20th-century façade of Valencia's town hall, Ayuntamiento, is marked by its symmetry, featuring domes with copper ceramic tiles at both ends. At the centre, you'll find the entrance, a platform for official appearances, and the flags of Valencia, Spain, and the EU, alongside the city's shield and clock. Behind this façade lies a much older 18th-century structure, that once served as a school. The town hall also houses the Historical City Museum, which is free to enter during office hours, offering an insight into Valencia's rich heritage.

Veles e Vents

Edificio Veles e Vents La Marina de València, 46024 Poblados Marítimos, veleseventsvalencia.es

The Veles e Vents ('Sails and Winds') building, designed by British architect David Chipperfield, is a striking four-level structure located in Valencia's marina. Originally built as the central hub for the 2007 America's Cup, it served as a base for race teams and offered spectators, including sponsors, prime views of the event from its rooftop. Today, the building is home to three renowned restaurants: La Sucursal, La Marítima, and Hoja Malabar. It is also a versatile space where concerts, meetings, and corporate events are hosted. Its minimalist design, with open terraces and panoramic views, makes it a key architectural and social landmark in Valencia.

Cathedral of Santa María

Plaça de l'Almoina, 46003 Ciutat Vella, catedraldevalencia.es

The Cathedral of Santa María was built over 600 years, starting in the 13th century. While its main structure is in the Valencian Gothic style, the cathedral incorporates elements from various architectural styles, including Romanesque, French Gothic, Renaissance, Baroque, and Neo-Classical. The cathedral is home to several treasures, most notably what Valencia claims to be the true Holy Grail, housed in a chapel immediately to the right upon entering. Additionally, the cathedral features two paintings by Goya, and frescos above the choir painted by Francesco Pagano and Paolo San Leocadio. Entrance is free on Sundays, while other days require a ticket, which includes an audio guide.

↓ CITY OF ARTS AND SCIENCES

↓ MERCADO COLÓN

Mercado Colón

*Carrer de Jorge Juan 19,
46004 L'Eixample*

The Mercado Colón, once a bustling market for fresh produce, has been transformed into a stylish food hall with lively bars and restaurants. The surrounding neighbourhood is filled with charming shops, making it a perfect spot for some retail therapy. After browsing, you can unwind with a refreshing drink in the sun. The building's façade showcases stunning Valencian Art Nouveau details on both sides, featuring mosaics showing Valencians in traditional dress surrounded by oranges and grapes. On closer inspection, you'll notice intricate designs of market staples such as chickens, rabbits, cows, crabs, scallops, and various fruits and vegetables.

Centro del Carmen

*Carrer del Museu 2-4,
46003 Ciutat Vella*

Located within a 13th-century convent, Centro del Carmen is a centre for contemporary art that creates a striking contrast with its historic setting. The peaceful courtyard is used for temporary exhibitions from time to time, and the most impressive space, the Salas Goerlich-Ferreres, features towering ceilings and Doric columns. Street artists are often invited to showcase their work within the walls of this former sanctuary. The centre also hosts a vibrant programme of performance art, including dance, theatre, and cinema. Best of all, entry is free, making it an accessible cultural hub for everyone to enjoy.

Water Tribunal of Valencia

*Plaça de la Verge 1,
46001 Ciutat Vella,
tribunaldelasaguas.org*

The Water Tribunal of the plain of Valencia, Tribunal de las Aguas, is an ancient court that has settled water disputes among farmers since the 10th century. Meeting every Thursday at noon outside the Apostles' Gate of Valencia Cathedral, it ensures the fair distribution of water from the Turia River to the surrounding irrigation channels. Composed of elected farmers, the tribunal hears cases orally and delivers quick, binding decisions. Remarkably, it operates without written records and remains one of the oldest still functioning courts in Europe. Its role is recognized by UNESCO as part of the Intangible Cultural Heritage of Humanity.

MUSEUMS

Science Museum

Avinguda del Professor López Piñero 7, 46013 Quatre Carreres, cac.es/museu-de-les-ciencies

The Science Museum in the City of Arts and Sciences is an interactive space designed for all ages, with a special focus on children and young adults eager to explore science, technology, and the environment. The ground floor features a cafeteria, museum shop, and ticket office. Visitors take the escalator to the first floor to access the exhibits.

IVAM

Carrer de Guillem de Castro 118, 46003 Ciutat Vella, ivam.es

Valencia's contemporary art museum IVAM (Institut Valencià d'Art Modern) features a permanent collection of works by Spanish sculptor Julio González and Valencian painter Ignacio Pinazo. In addition to its core collection, the museum hosts an ever-changing selection of fascinating exhibitions by emerging as well as established artists. The museum's restaurant Mascaraque offers a delightful and affordably priced *menu del día* for lunch.

MuVIM

Carrer de Quevedo 10, 46001 Ciutat Vella, muvim.es

Museu Valencià de la Il·lustració i de la Modernitat focuses on the evolution of modern thought from the Enlightenment to today. Opened in 2001, it features immersive exhibitions on intellectual history, graphic design, and communication. Designed by architect Guillermo Vázquez Consuegra, MuVIM also hosts educational programmes and debates, making it a cultural hub for exploring modernity and its influence on society.

Hortensia Herrero Art Centre

Carrer del Mar 31, 46003 Ciutat Vella, cahh.es

Within the walls of the restored Palacio de Valeriola, you'll find a cultural space dedicated to contemporary art: Hortensia Herrero Art Centre. Founded by philanthropist and businesswoman Herrero Chacón, it showcases international and Spanish art, including her private collection. The artists include Jaume Plensa, Mat Collishaw, Tony Cragg, Julio González, David Hockney, Anselm Kiefer, and Joan Miró.

↓ MUVIM

↓ FUNDACIÓN BANCAJA

L'Etno

*Carrer de la Corona 36,
46003 Ciutat Vella,
letno.dival.es*

L'Etno, or Museum of Ethnology, offers an engaging exploration of Valencian culture, history, and traditions. With interactive exhibits on rural life, festivals, and craftsmanship, it presents a modern take on local heritage and the region's cultural identity. Located in La Beneficència Cultural Centre, it also hosts temporary exhibitions and family-friendly workshops.

Museo Ciencias Naturales

*Carrer del General Elio,
46010 La Zaidía*

While visiting the Museo Ciencias Naturales, you will travel through the Earth's geological periods, highlighting over four billion years of evolutionary change evidenced by fossils. This journey through the palaeontology of the Valencian Community enhances your understanding of the region's changing landscapes and ecosystems. It explores the coexistence of extinct animals and early humans in rock shelters, showing the rich biodiversity that once thrived in our territory thousands of years ago.

Museo Mundo de Ilusiones

*Carrer del Mestre Clavé 3, 46001 Ciutat Vella,
museomundodeilusiones-valencia.com*

Are you in for a fascinating experience that plays with your perception through stunning optical illusions? Visit Museo Mundo de Ilusiones. Each room presents a unique surreal scene that challenges your sense of reality and transports you to another world. Located in the city centre, this museum is perfect for creating memorable experiences, capturing Instagram-worthy moments, and enjoying a fun afternoon with friends.

Museo Histórico de Valencia

Carrer València 42, 46920 L'Olivereta

You'll find the Museo Histórico de Valencia near Jardín del Turía and Bioparc. Often overlooked by tourists because of its location, this museum offers valuable insights into Valencian history. The underground dungeons, illuminated by dim lighting, create a dramatic and sinister atmosphere reminiscent of medieval times, allowing visitors to feel as though they are stepping back into the past. It's worth a visit for a deeper understanding of the region's heritage.

Àgora - CaixaForum

Carrer d'Eduardo Primo Yúfera 1A, 46013 Quatre Carreres, caixaforum.org/es/valencia

Àgora - CaixaForum in the City of Arts and Sciences is not to be missed. This striking cobalt blue structure standing 70 metres tall, was once an event space that hosted the Open 500 ATP tennis tournament for six years. Today, it serves as a cultural centre featuring a variety of rotating exhibitions and performances that travel to CaixaForums in other major Spanish cities.

Fallas Museum

Plaça de Montolivet 4, 46006 Quatre Carreres es/valencia

Las Fallas is Valencia's largest celebration, taking place in March, with the grand finale on the 19th. At the Fallas Museum, you can explore various aspects of this rich tradition, including *mascletà* (the unique firecracker display), *falleras* (women in traditional attire), local music, folk dancing, the community's passion for making paella on the streets, and the artistry involved in creating the impressive statues that are displayed and ultimately burnt on the final night.

L'Almoina

Plaça de Dècim Juni Brut, 46003 Ciutat Vella

The archaeological museum L'Almoina showcases Roman remains from ancient Valencia, dating back to before the Common Era. The planned extension of the Basilica was halted due to the significant treasures discovered at the site. After years of excavations that also revealed Visigoth and Moorish artifacts, the site was ultimately covered and transformed into a museum for the public to explore and appreciate.

Museo de la Seda

Carrer del Hospital 7, 46001 Ciutat Vella, museodelasedavalencia.com

The Museo de la Seda is the silk museum located in the Colegio del Arte Mayor de la Seda. Silk arrived in Valencia in the 15th century through the Silk Road. Valencian farmers learned how to cultivate silk themselves by growing mulberry trees and raising silk caterpillars. Over the years, silk became a vital commodity. The museum provides insights into the lives of the farmers, the silk production process, and the history of silk fashion in Valencia.

Fundación Bancaja

Plaça de Tetuan 23, 46003 Ciutat Vella, fundacionbancaja.es

The historic building Fundación Bancaja houses the cultural foundation dedicated to promoting art and social initiatives. It hosts a variety of events, including exhibitions and workshops, showing both contemporary and historical works. The foundation features pieces from prominent artists such as Andy Warhol, Pablo Picasso, Manolo Valdés, Joaquín Sorolla, Fernando Botero, and Eduardo Chillida.

Palacio del Marqués de dos Aguas

Carrer del Poeta Querol 2, 46002 Ciutat Vella

The National Ceramic Museum is housed in the Palacio del Marqués de dos Aguas. Valencia has a rich history of ceramic production, with nearby villages like Manises and Paterna still home to workshops for ceramic tiles and pottery. The museum features a diverse collection of local ceramics as well as pieces from all over the world. The Rococo palace has been beautifully restored, showcasing 18th-century furniture throughout its spaces.

Museo del Patriarca

Carrer de la Nau 2, 46003 Ciutat Vella, patriarcavalencia.es

The Real Colegio Seminario del Corpus Christi was a Catholic school and seminary established in the early 17th century. The Museo del Patriarca is housed within these historic buildings, which include a church, a smaller chapel, a Renaissance cloister, living quarters, classrooms, and a library. The museum's collection features paintings by renowned artists such as Caravaggio, El Greco, Pinazo, Benlliure, Ribalta, and Van der Teyden.

↓ MUVIM

↓ FALLAS MUSEUM

STREET ART

Okuda San Miguel

Carrer de Sant Vicent Màrtir 171, 46007 Extramurs

A striking mural by Okuda San Miguel, a Spanish street artist known for his colourful, geometric style, is featured prominently at Sorolla Station. His vibrant works blend surrealism with urban influences, using bold shapes and colours to create dreamlike, kaleidoscopic images. His mural at Sorolla Station adds an artistic touch to this bustling transportation hub, inviting travellers into his vivid, imaginative world.

Escif

Passatge Doctor Serra 25, 46004 L'Eixample

Escif is a Valencian street artist famous for his minimalist, thought-provoking murals that often include social and political commentary. His mural at Passatge Doctor Serra is no exception, presenting work depicting children working as slaves in the textile industry. Escif's approach tends to be subtle and conceptual, often blending into the urban environment while provoking deep thoughts. He is also referred to as 'El Banksy Valenciano'.

Hyuro

Carrer Poble Nou de la Mar, 46011 Poblats Marítims

The seaside neighbourhood of Cabanyal features works by Hyuro, an Argentine-born artist who lived and worked in Valencia for much of her career. Her murals, often monochromatic and deeply symbolic, focus on themes of human vulnerability, social justice, and the struggle for equality. Hyuro's street art in Cabanyal reflects both personal and collective experiences, creating narratives that connect with the local community.

Alfonso Calza

Carrer de Moret 6, 46003 Ciutat Vella

The celebrated Spanish poet Gustavo Adolfo Bécquer is honoured in the piece *Beso de Valencia*. The mural depicts a romantic kiss, inspired by Bécquer's statement: 'el alma que hablar puede con los ojos, también puede besar con la mirada' (the soul that can speak with its eyes can also kiss with its gaze), and has become one of the most photographed pieces in the city. You can find it on Carrer de Moret, also known as 'Calle de los Colores', as the street is filled with colourful murals.

Alfonso Yuste Navarro

Carrer del Museu 11, 46003 Ciutat Vella

Casa de los Gatos (House of Cats) is a quirky installation created by Alfonso Yuste Navarro. This miniature house, nestled in the wall of an empty plot in the district El Carmen, is a tribute to the neighbourhood's stray cats. Navarro's playful, detailed work creates a whimsical surprise for passersby, adding a unique and charming touch to the city's urban landscape.

PichiAvo, Barbiturikills, Deih XLF & Toni Espinar

Carrer de Foios 9, 46001 Ciutat Vella

On Plaza de la Botxa, you can find an impressive collaboration between multiple renowned street artists: PichiAvo, known for their fusion of classical and graffiti styles; Barbiturikills, who blends pop culture with bold, colourful elements; Deih XLF, recognised for his sci-fi-inspired, intricate murals; and Toni Espinar, whose political and social art speaks to contemporary issues. Together, their works transform the plaza into a visually dynamic space that celebrates modern street art.

Julieta XLF

Avinguda de Blasco Ibáñez 30, 46010 El Pla del Real

The prominent Valencian Street artist Julieta XLF has adorned the Facultad de Filosofía y Ciencias de la Educación with her signature style: colourful characters that often explore themes of femininity, nature, and fantasy. Her joyful, vibrant murals bring life and imagination to the university space, making it an inspiring place for students and visitors alike. She was once a Fine Arts student there and holds a master's degree in illustration.

Felipe Pantone

Carrer de Joan Verdeguer 16, 46024 Poblats Marítims

Las Naves, a cultural and innovation space in Valencia, features work by Felipe Pantone, a globally recognised artist known for his futuristic, digital-inspired aesthetic. Pantone blends vibrant colour gradients with glitchy, pixelated forms, often incorporating optical illusions and technological elements. His murals at Las Naves reflect his signature blend of art and technology, creating a visually stimulating environment that complements the centre's forward-thinking mission.

CINEMA

Most cinemas in Valencia show films that are dubbed: not ideal for foreigners, even when they are fluent in Spanish. However, a few cinemas offer films in the original language. Try to find films that are marked V.O. (original version), V.O.S.E. (original version with Spanish subtitles). Don't confuse the latter with V.O.E.S.I. (Spanish version with English subtitles).

Cines Babel

Carrer de Vicent Sancho Tello 10,
46021 El Pla del Real,
cinesalbatrosbabel.com

Known for its cosy setting, Cines Babel specialises in independent, international, and art-house films. Most movies are shown in the original version. The cinema also hosts small film festivals and other cultural events.

Cine Yelmo

Avinguda de Tirso de Molina 16, 46015 Campanar, yelmocines.es

Located in the modern Mercado de Campanar complex, Cine Yelmo is a large multiplex screening a wide selection of blockbusters and 3D films. Some are available in the original version.

Cines Lys

Passatge de Russafa 3,
46002 Ciutat Vella,
cineslys.com

Cines Lys is centrally located and features both mainstream and independent films. Some are shown in the original version. The ticket office is outside, and film times are clearly displayed.

La Filmoteca

Plaça de l'Ajuntament 17, 46002 Ciutat Vella

Housed in the Rialto, an Art Deco building from 1939, La Filmoteca specialises in classic, cultural, and international films, documentaries, retrospectives, short films, and theatre.

IMAX L'Hemisfèric

Avinguda del Professor López Piñero 3, 46013 Quatre Carreres, cac.es/hemisferic

Situated in the City of Arts & Sciences, the IMAX L'Hemisfèric offers an immersive visual experience on a wide screen, with some films shown in 3D. Most films are documentaries or educational. Visitors use futuristic headphones to select their preferred language.

↓ IMAX L'HEMISFÈRIC

FESTIVALS

Las Fallas

fallas.com

March is the month of Las Fallas, with festivities intensifying as 19th March approaches. Streets come alive with paella cooking, fireworks, flower processions, pop-up dance parties, and towering statues displayed in every neighbourhood. This vibrant festival, rooted in tradition, draws large crowds from across Spain and is gaining international recognition.

Feria de Julio

granferiavalencia.com

Feria de Julio is Valencia's summer festival, designed to encourage people to stay in the city despite the heat. Held in July, it features open-air concerts in Viveros Park, the colourful Batalla de Flores ('flower battle'), fairs, the selection of *falleras*, and street theatre across various neighbourhoods.

9 d'Octubre

9th October marks Valencia Region Day, celebrating Jaime I's recapture of the city from Moorish rule in 1238. The day begins with an official ceremony in which the Valencian flag is brought to Jaime I's statue, alongside flower offerings. Later, participants in medieval Moorish and Christian costumes parade through the city centre. On the same day, San Donís, Valencia's version of Valentine's Day, is celebrated, and couples exchange marzipan and scarves.

Halloween & Día de Todos los Santos

On 31st October, Valencia celebrates Halloween with spooky costumes and themed parties at bars, restaurants, and clubs throughout the city. The next day, 1st November, is Día de Todos los Santos, when families visit cemeteries to lay flowers on graves. Bakeries sell marzipan treats known as *huesos de santo*, 'saint's bones'.

La Tomatina Buñol

latomatina.info

The small town of Buñol, forty kilometres from Valencia, hosts the world-famous La Tomatina on the last Wednesday of August. Each year, thousands of people from around the globe join this massive tomato fight, with over 120,000 kilos of tomatoes used in the hour-long event. The fight attracts around 20,000 participants and has become a global sensation.

↓ LAS FALLAS

Festival de les Arts

festivaldelesarts.com

Festival de les Arts is a two-day music festival held in the iconic City of Arts and Sciences complex. The festival features a mix of indie, pop, rock, and electronic music, with a strong lineup of Spanish and international bands. The stunning architectural backdrop of the venue makes it a unique cultural experience. The festival also features art exhibitions, food trucks, and activities related to visual and performing arts.

FIB Festival Internacional Benicàssim

fiberfib.com

As one of Europe's biggest mid-July summer music festivals, FIB attracts thousands of international visitors to the coastal town of Benicàssim. The festival runs for four days and features a mix of indie, pop, electronic, and rock acts. International headliners perform alongside Spanish bands, making it a favourite for music lovers. Its beachside location allows festivalgoers to enjoy music as well as the Mediterranean coastline.

Rototom Sunsplash

rototomsunsplash.com

Rototom Sunsplash, mid-August in Benicàssim, is one of Europe's largest reggae festivals, promoting peace, equality, and social justice. The festival lasts for a week and offers much more than just music. In addition to performances by leading reggae artists, it also features workshops, talks, exhibitions, yoga, and cultural events. The festival is known for its friendly, inclusive atmosphere, attracting a global community of reggae fans.

THINGS TO DO

Yoga in the Park

yogawithjennison.com

Jennison, originally from the U.S., now lives in Valencia with her husband and son. She hosts yoga classes in Jardín del Turía, welcoming a mostly female group but always encourages all visitors to join in. When the moon is full, she offers magical night yoga sessions on the beach.

Free Walking Tours

spainfreetours.com/en/tours/valencia

These tip-based walking tours let you explore Valencia's historical centre. Choose from a variety of tours, such as the Street Art tour or the Essential Valencia tour. Guides are easy to spot in their orange jumpers, holding umbrellas.

Hiking in the Mountains

nuestra-aventura.com

Stefan is an experienced mountain guide with a deep love for the outdoors. He takes groups on hikes tailored to their skill level, leading you through his favourite areas, including mountains, waterfalls, and lush forests.

Language Exchange

valencialanguageexchange.com

Looking to practice Spanish and meet new people? The language exchange is perfect! With events nearly every day, participants meet in local pubs to speak English with native speakers of Spanish and improve their language skills, and Spanish speakers to practise their English.

Pub Crawl

tourmeout.com/actividad/pub-crawl-valencia

Join a local guide as they take you to four of the best bars and pubs in Valencia, where locals love to hang out. A fun night out with fellow young travellers is guaranteed!

City Bike Tour

bikeguyvlc.com

Luke, known as 'the bike guy', offers humorous and engaging bike tours through Valencia. The tour starts in the city centre and ends at the beach, where you can relax and enjoy a meal after the ride.

Surf, Wind Surf, Wing Foil or Paddle Surf

oceanrepublik.com

Ocean Republik is led by a laid-back team of surf enthusiasts who offer a range of water sports experiences adapted to the wind and wave conditions. Whether you're surfing, windsurfing, wing foiling, or paddle surfing, you can enjoy these thrilling activities almost year-round on the Mediterranean.

Tapas Tour

toursinvalencia.com/nl/tours/tapas-tour

Join a tapas tour through Barrio del Carmen to discover

traditional dishes, the best tapas bars, and to learn about the history of tapas culture. Gabriel or one of the other friendly guides will lead you on this flavourful journey.

Ivan Wines

ivanwines.com

Ivan is an oenologist and an expert in Spanish wines. He offers the finest wine tastings in town, blending his deep knowledge with an ever-evolving source of inspiration. Each experience introduces you to exceptional wines, highlighting a unique region or a specific grape variety.

Flor de Luna

flordelunaofficial.com

Jessica, founder of Flor de Luna, hosts workshops where participants create artistic arrangements using dried flowers and organic materials, inspired by Nordic aesthetics. Sessions include crafting flower crowns, bouquets, and themed decor for holidays, weddings, and baby showers.

Picnic in the Park

Treat yourself to delicious food from Mercado Central and have a relaxing picnic in Jardín del Turia. The market offers the finest local delicacies, and the park provides the perfect setting to enjoy them.

Painting and Wine

theartwinehouse.com

At The Art Wine House, you'll paint with neon colours while sipping on wine. It's a fun and relaxed class, and no artistic experience is needed! Perfect for anyone looking to unleash their creativity.

FAMOUS PEOPLE

Santiago Calatrava

The internationally acclaimed architect and engineer Santiago Calatrava, known for his avant-garde, futuristic designs, was born in Benimàmet, Valencia. His works include the Turning Torso in Sweden, the Milwaukee Art Museum, and the Oculus in New York City. Renowned for his use of white concrete and steel, his work emphasises fluid, organic forms, often inspired by the human body and nature, making him a global architectural icon.

Carmen Alborch

Born in Castellón but deeply connected to Valencia, Carmen Alborch was a pioneering feminist, cultural leader, and politician. She served as Spain's Minister of Culture from 1993 to 1996 and was a fierce advocate for gender equality. Alborch also directed the Valencia Institute of Modern Art (IVAM) and was a member of the Valencian Parliament, tirelessly promoting women's rights and cultural initiatives throughout her life.

Joaquín Sorolla

One of Spain's most celebrated impressionist painters, Joaquín Sorolla was born in Valencia in 1863. Known for his masterful use of light, his work often depicted the Mediterranean coast, Valencian landscapes, and everyday life in Spain. His famous painting *Walk on the Beach* shows his profound connection to Valencia's seaside. The Museo Sorolla in Madrid showcases much of his work, though Valencia remains a central theme in his art.

David Ferrer

David Ferrer is a retired Spanish professional tennis player born in Xàbia, Valencia, in 1982. Known for his consistency, speed, and fighting spirit, he reached a career-high ranking as World No. 3. Ferrer won 27 ATP titles, played in the 2013 French Open final, and helped Spain secure three Davis Cup titles. Revered for his sportsmanship, he is one of tennis's greats.

Almudena Muñoz

Born in Valencia, Almudena Muñoz made history by winning Olympic gold in judo at the 1992 Barcelona Games in the −52 kg category. She became one of the first Spanish women to achieve such a prestigious honour in martial arts, cementing her place as a trailblazer for Spanish athletes. Her achievements brought attention to judo in Spain, and she remains an important figure in the Valencian sports community.

Juan Luis Vives

The prominent Renaissance humanist, philosopher, and educator Juan Luis Vives was born in Valencia in 1493. A contemporary of Erasmus, Vives was a pioneer in educational theory and advocated for women's education and social reform. His influential works, such as *De Anima et Vita*, had a profound impact on European intellectual life. His legacy is honoured in Valencia, where his contributions to education and philosophy are widely celebrated.

Patsy Ferran

A rising star in British theatre and film, Patsy Ferran was born in Valencia and raised in the U.K. Known for her performances in the West End, including her award-winning role in *Summer and Smoke*,

Ferran has gained recognition for her unique talent and versatility. Though she moved to the U.K. at a young age, her Valencian roots remain an important part of her identity.

Miguel Bernardeau

Remember Guzmán in the popular Netflix series *Elite*? He was played by Valenciano Miguel Bernardeau. As the son of actress Ana Duato, Bernardeau grew up immersed in the entertainment world. He has since become a prominent figure in Spanish television and film, representing Valencia's contribution to modern Spanish pop culture on the global stage.

Rodrigo de Borja

Born in Xàtiva, Valencia, Rodrigo de Borja, later known as Pope Alexander VI, was one of the most controversial popes of the Renaissance. As head of the powerful Borgia family, he was infamous for his political manoeuvring, nepotism, and scandalous papacy. Despite his contentious legacy, his Valencian roots are still a point of historical pride, with his impact on European history undeniable.

Begoña Rodrigo

The Valencia-born chef Begoña Rodrigo gained national fame after winning Spain's first season of *Top Chef*. She runs the highly acclaimed La Salita, known for its innovative, locally inspired cuisine. Rodrigo focuses on using Valencian ingredients with a modern twist, making her a key figure in the city's growing gastronomic scene. Her work highlights Valencia's culinary richness and creativity.

Luis García Berlanga

Considered one of Spain's most influential filmmakers, the Valencian Luis García Berlanga is known for his sharp, satirical films. He addressed political and social issues during Franco's dictatorship with humour and nuance. Films like *¡Bienvenido, Mister Marshall!* and *El Verdugo* are now classics of Spanish cinema. His legacy is celebrated in Valencia, as his contributions to Spanish film are an integral part of the cultural heritage.

Escif

A Valencia-based street artist known for his minimalist, politically charged murals. His works, often painted on public walls, address themes like capitalism, environmentalism, and social justice. Escif's art has gained international attention, but many of his most iconic works are located around Valencia. His thought-provoking murals have turned the city into an open-air gallery, merging art and activism.

Elisabet Benavent

One of the most successful contemporary romance authors is Elisabet Benavent, born in Gandía, Valenciana. Her *Valeria* series, which has been adapted into a successful Netflix show, captures the complexities of modern relationships, often set against the backdrop of Spanish life. Benavent's witty, relatable storytelling has earned her a large following, and she continues to represent Valencia's vibrant literary scene.

Hortensia Herrero Chacón

A successful businesswoman and philanthropist. As vice-president of the Mercadona supermarket chain, Herrero has played a key role in its growth. She is also known for her philanthropy, especially in the arts, through the Hortensia Herrero Foundation, which funds cultural projects and restores historical landmarks in Valencia, including the San Nicolás Church and the Palau de Valeriola.

FILMS & SERIES IN AND ABOUT VALENCIA

Tomorrowland (Project T, 2015)

A futuristic adventure in which a teen discovers a mysterious pin that transports her to a utopian world, Tomorrowland (City of Arts and Sciences). She teams up with a disillusioned inventor (George Clooney) to uncover secrets of this advanced society and save Earth from destruction. Together, they fight to restore hope and innovation in a world consumed by pessimism. Streaming on Disney+.

El Embarcadero (The Pier, 2019/2020)

An architect's life is turned upside down when her husband commits suicide. She uncovers his secret double life with another woman. Torn between grief and curiosity, she embarks on a journey to understand his choices, forming an unexpected bond with his lover, blending mystery and emotional self-discovery. The scenes are mostly shot at the natural park of Albufera ten kilometres south of the city of Valencia. Streaming on Prime Video.

Westworld (2020)

Set in a high-tech amusement park where android 'hosts' cater to guests' fantasies, HBO's *Westworld* explores the dark consequences of artificial intelligence and human desires. As hosts gain self-awareness, they challenge their creators, leading to philosophical questions about free will, identity, and the boundaries between human and machine. For the third season, the City of Arts and Sciences was one of the filming locations.

Doctor Who – Smile (2017)

In BBC's *Doctor Who: Smile*, the Doctor and Bill travel to a futuristic human colony (City of Arts & Sciences) where robots, called Vardies, use emojis to communicate. However, the colony has turned deadly as the Vardies eliminate anyone who shows sadness. The Doctor uncovers the truth behind the robots' programming and saves the colonists from a tragic misunderstanding.

Respira (Breathless, 2024)

The hospital series *Respira* is set in a public hospital in Valencia. Alongside various medical cases, the show delves into the hospital's underlying political issues. Poor working conditions and low wages lead to a strike by doctors and medical staff. The series also addresses challenges like the severe Valencian rains, drug-related problems, and suicide, offering a layered narrative of healthcare and social struggles. You can watch *Respira* on Netflix.

El Cid (1961)

The heroic historical figure Rodrigo Díaz de Vivar (Charlton Heston), known as El Cid, defends Spain from Moorish invaders. After reconquering Valencia, he becomes the city's ruler, protecting it from further attacks. Torn between his love for Jimena (Sophia Loren) and his duty, El Cid rises as a noble warrior, uniting Spain.

Vivir dos veces (Live Twice, Love Once, 2019)

Emilio, an aging man diagnosed with Alzheimer's, embarks on a road trip with his daughter and granddaughter to find his first love before his memory fades. This heartwarming dramedy on Netflix explores themes of family, love, and living life to the fullest, even in the face of inevitable loss.

Citadel (2023)

A global espionage series following elite agents of the fallen independent spy agency Citadel, starring Richard Madden and Priyanka Chopra. As they try to rebuild their organisation, they face enemies with immense power, grappling with betrayal, secrets, and personal stakes. It's a high-octane, fast-paced thriller full of twists, action, and international intrigue you can watch on Prime Video.

Uncharted (2022)

Based on the popular video game, this action-adventure follows treasure hunter Nathan Drake and his mentor Sully as they embark on a globetrotting quest to find a long-lost fortune. Filmed in stunning locations like Jávea, Comunidad Valenciana, they face dangerous rivals, cryptic clues, and ancient mysteries in this thrilling treasure hunt.

Game of Thrones (2016)

The medieval town of Peñíscola, Comunidad Valenciana, serves as the backdrop for Meereen in Game of Thrones, first seen in the 4th episode of the 6th season. In the series, Daenerys Targaryen's struggle for power unfolds in this ancient, exotic city. Peñíscola's dramatic landscapes and historical architecture contribute to the epic fantasy setting of political intrigue and deadly battles.

El Silencio del Pantano (The Silence of the Marsh, 2019)

A crime novelist researching corruption in Valencia becomes entangled in real-life criminal activity. As fiction and reality blur, the writer's dark, violent tendencies surface. This psychological thriller explores moral ambiguity and the consequences of crossing ethical lines in pursuit of a gripping story.

La Boda de Rosa (Rosa's Wedding, 2020)

Rosa, a middle-aged woman overwhelmed by family obligations, decides to take control of her life by marrying herself. This feel-good Spanish comedy on Netflix addresses self-care, empowerment, and the importance of prioritising personal happiness, as Rosa breaks free from societal expectations and her family's constant demands.

Dolor y Gloria (Pain and Glory, 2019)

Directed by Pedro Almodóvar, this semi-autobiographical drama follows aging film director Salvador Mallo (Antonio Banderas), who reflects on his life, past loves, and creative struggles. As he grapples with physical pain and emotional turmoil, the film explores memory, art, and reconciliation with the past, blending poignant storytelling with vivid visuals.

See You on Venus (2023)

Two teenagers, Mia and Kyle, embark on a life-changing journey to Spain in search of Mia's birth mother. Along the way, they form a deep emotional connection and grapple with love, identity, and loss. This romantic drama captures the beauty of first love and the bittersweet reality of life's uncertainties.

Lo que Sabemos (What We Know, 2021)

In this coming-of-age drama, a group of friends faces life-changing decisions as they navigate young adulthood in a small Valencian town. *Lo que Sabemos* delicately explores themes of love, friendship, and personal growth, as each character struggles with their desires, insecurities, and the paths their lives may take.

BOOKS IN & ABOUT VALENCIA

A Death in Valencia – Jason Webster

This crime novel follows Chief Inspector Max Cámara as he investigates the murder of a controversial chef in the heart of Valencia. As he delves deeper, he uncovers a web of corruption, political tensions, and urban redevelopment. The story offers a vivid depiction of Valencia's streets and its culture clashes, all while building a tense, thrilling mystery.

The Sun Also Rises – Ernest Hemingway

This classic novel depicts the post-WWI 'Lost Generation' as a group of them travels from Paris to Spain, including Valencia. Focusing on the disillusioned expatriates, bullfights, and the Pamplona fiesta, it captures the restless energy of its characters as they search for meaning in a world forever changed by war.

Arroz y Tartana (Rice and Cart) – Vicente Blasco Ibáñez

Set in 19th-century Valencia, this novel portrays a once-wealthy widow, Doña Manuela, striving to maintain her social status as she faces financial ruin. Through her struggles, the story delves into themes of pride, tradition, and social mobility, offering a rich portrayal of Valencian society during a period of economic transition.

Valencia With Love – B.J. Smyth

In this romance novel, a young woman relocates to Valencia for a fresh start, finding not only a new city but also unexpected love. As she explores the beauty and culture of the city, she discovers that sometimes, life

and love can flourish in the most unexpected places. A heartwarming journey set in beautiful Valencia.

Murder in Valencia – Roy Lewis

This mystery novel features Detective Eric Ward investigating a British expat's murder in Valencia. As Ward delves into the case, he uncovers layers of deceit and dark secrets within the expat community. The novel offers an intriguing blend of crime-solving, the complexities of human relationships, and the charm of Valencia's setting.

The Lord of Valencia – Griff Hosker

A historical fiction novel set in medieval Spain, it follows Rodrigo Diaz de Vivar, also known as El Cid, and his journey to become the Lord of Valencia. This epic tale explores his battles, political struggles, and personal challenges as he attempts to carve out a kingdom in a land divided by war.

Valencia – James Nulick

A haunting, modern novel. *Valencia* explores themes of isolation, identity, and disillusionment in contemporary society. The book weaves between multiple characters' lives, portraying their existential struggles and search for meaning. Nulick's writing is stark and introspective, blending the desolation of modern life with fleeting moments of connection.

The Borgias: The Hidden History – G.J. Meyer

This historical account delves into the controversial lives of the Borgia family, infamous for their corruption, scandal, and power within the Catholic Church. Meyer sheds light on the political manoeuvring and intrigue surrounding figures like Pope Alexander VI and Lucrezia Borgia, offering a nuanced look at one of history's most notorious families.

The Scent of Lemon Leaves – Clara Sánchez

In this emotional novel, Sandra, a young woman, meets an elderly couple with a dark Nazi past in the sunlit region of Valencia. As Sandra uncovers their hidden secrets, she must confront moral dilemmas and the complexities of memory, guilt, and justice. The novel blends suspense, historical reflection, and psychological depth.

The Perfume Garden – Kate Lord Brown

Set in both contemporary times and during the Spanish Civil War, this novel follows Emma Temple, a perfume maker, who inherits a house in Valencia. As she renovates it, she uncovers her grandmother's hidden past and forbidden love during the war. A dual narrative that intertwines love, war, and the healing power of scent.

Un Cuento Perfecto (A Perfect Story) – Elísabet Benavent

This romance novel tells the story of Margot, a successful woman questioning her life, and David, a young man living a simpler, more spontaneous existence. As their paths cross, they embark on a journey of self-discovery and emotional growth, exploring the complexities of love, relationships, and what it means to live a 'perfect' life. Netflix made a miniseries of this book.

FUN FACTS

Agua de Valencia

The cocktail Agua de Valencia was first mixed in 1959 by bartender Constante Gil at Café Madrid in Valencia. Initially ordered by some Basque travellers, when the bar had run out of the best cava from the Basque Country. The drink combines a cava (Spanish sparkling wine), fresh Valencian orange juice, vodka, and gin. Café de Madrid reopened its doors some years ago, but you can order it at any Valencian terrace nowadays.

Europe's narrowest house

Located on Plaza de Lope de Vega, Valencia boasts Europe's narrowest house, measuring only 107 centimetres at its front. This five-storey building, though tiny from the outside, cleverly expands towards the back. It's become a quirky attraction in the city, and though no longer residential, it draws curious visitors and has inspired local legends about its unique design.

A heraldic symbol: the bat

The bat appears in Valencia's coat of arms, a symbol dating back to the reign of King Jaime I. According to legend, a bat helped the king during his conquest of Valencia in 1238 by alerting him to an approaching enemy. Since then, the bat has been a significant emblem of the city, representing protection, vigilance, and the historical triumph of Valencia.

Quedarse a la luna de Valencia

The Valencian saying 'quedarse a la luna de Valencia' ('to stay at

the moon of Valencia'), means 'to be left stranded' or 'to be disappointed'. It originated in medieval times. If travellers arrived after Valencia's city gates had closed for the night, they were left outside, spending the night under the moonlight. Over time, this became a popular expression throughout Spain for people who miss out or are left waiting for something.

Monsters of Valencia

Valencian folklore includes mythical figures used to scare misbehaving children. L'Home del Sac ('the sack man') supposedly kidnaps naughty children in his sack, while Butoni is a bogeyman who lurks in dark places. Banyeta is a small horned devil, and L'Home dels Nassols visits on 31st December, with just one nose after starting with 365 and losing a nose each day. These characters are still part of local storytelling traditions.

The Holy Grail in Valencia

Valencia's Cathedral is believed to house the Holy Grail, the sacred cup used by Christ at the Last Supper. The Chapel of the Holy Chalice within the cathedral holds a revered relic made of agate, believed by some scholars to be the original grail. The cup has drawn pilgrims and visitors for centuries, making it one of the city's most spiritually significant treasures.

UNESCO World Heritage Sites

Valencia is home to three UNESCO-recognised cultural treasures. Built between 1482 and 1533, Valencia's Silk Exchange (La Lonja de la Seda) is a late Gothic architectural masterpiece originally used for silk trading. Tribunal de las Aguas is Europe's oldest water court, meeting weekly since Moorish times to resolve irrigation disputes. Las Fallas Festival, a fiery, artistic celebration held every March, culminates in the burning of enormous statues known as *fallas*.

Super healthy

The refreshing Valencian drink made from tiger nuts is called *horchata de chufa*. This ancient beverage is known for its health benefits, being rich in antioxidants, fibres, and essential vitamins. It is considered to aid digestion, lower cholesterol, and boost energy. Traditionally enjoyed with *fartons* (sweet pastries), horchata is a staple of Valencian cuisine and is especially popular during summer.

Cornucopia

The ancient Roman city of Valentia, founded in 138 BCE, had the cornucopia (horn of plenty) as its symbol. This emblem represented abundance, fertility, and prosperity, reflecting the city's importance as a trading hub and agricultural centre during Roman times. Valencia's strategic location on the Mediterranean ensured its growth into a thriving, wealthy city.

A 10-kilometre park

After the disastrous Turia River Flood of 1957, the river was rerouted to prevent a reoccurrence. The old riverbed was transformed into Jardín del Turia, a 10-kilometre-long green space running through the heart of Valencia. Now one of Europe's largest urban parks, it features bicycle paths, playgrounds, sports facilities, and cultural landmarks. In 2024, Valencia was named Green Capital of Europe for its commitment to sustainability and urban greenery.

PHOTO SPOTS

L'Umbracle

Avinguda del Professor López Piñero 5, 46013 Quatre Carreres

L'Umbracle is a beautiful garden located beneath the white arches in the City of Arts and Sciences. As you walk through, you're greeted with a stunning contrast of lush greenery, vibrant plants, and the white arches set against the blue sky. The garden features orange trees, palm trees, and rosemary bushes. Another section of L'Umbracle operates as a club during summer, opening at midnight for nighttime entertainment.

Puente de las Flores

Jardín del Turía

Jardín del Turía is crossed by nineteen bridges, each with its own unique character and history. One of the more modern bridges is Puente de las Flores, designed by Santiago Calatrava, the architect behind the City of Arts and Sciences. Calatrava designed a total of five bridges over the park. The highlight of Puente de las Flores is the vibrant geraniums that bloom year-round, adding a splash of colour to the bridge.

El Miguelete tower

Plaça de la Reina, 46001 Ciutat Vella

The bell tower of Valencia Cathedral, El Miguelete, is named after its largest bell, first rung on Saint Michael's Day. To reach the top and enjoy stunning panoramic views, you'll need to climb a narrow spiral staircase with

↓ VALENCIA CATHEDRAL

↓ PUENTE DE LAS FLORES

207 medieval steps. From the top, you'll look over the rooftops of the city centre, and on clear days, you can see the Mediterranean Sea, the Mestalla football stadium, and the City of Arts and Sciences.

Sunrise at the Malvarrosa beach

Paseo Marítimo 14, 46011 Poblats Marítims

In Valencia, the sun rises over the sea and sets over land. During the summer, waking up early offers the chance to witness a breath-taking sunrise over Malvarrosa Beach. It's a peaceful time, perfect for a morning jog or a relaxing walk along the shoreline, as the beach remains quiet at dawn.

Museo de Bellas Artes' pink courtyard

Carrer de Sant Pius V 9, 46010 La Saïdia

The Museo de Bellas Artes (Museum of Fine Arts) houses an impressive collection of nearly 2,000 paintings and sculptures by masters such as El Greco, Goya, and Velázquez, ranging from the 14th to the 17th century. Don't miss the charming pink and blue courtyard inside, an ideal spot for photography.

El Cabañal

The devastating fire of 1875 destroyed many traditional fisherman's homes known as *barracas* in the Cabañal neighbourhood. New houses were built for the local families. These two-storey homes are decorated with colourful ceramic tiles in various patterns. Many of these listed historical houses have been recently restored to preserve their unique charm.

Inside the opera house Palau de les Arts

Avinguda del Professor López Piñero 1, 46013 Quatre Carreres

The Palau de les Arts, the opera house within the City of Arts and Sciences, is not only photogenic from the outside but also offers intriguing architectural details inside. Highlights include the spiral staircase, which resembles a snail's shell, and the cobalt blue ceramic door handles in the shape of human figures. The view from the eighth floor is also spectacular.

The Botanic Garden

Carrer de Quart 80, 46008 Extramurs

Valencia's Botanic Garden is home to a diverse range of plants and trees that bloom nearly year-round, as well as a friendly population of cats. These cats are well cared for with food and medical attention, and they are often seen lounging around the garden, posing for photos with visitors amidst the greenery.

Marina Real Juan Carlos I

Carrer del Moll de la Duana, 46024 Poblats Marítims

Valencia's marina, Real Juan Carlos I, is a relaxing spot for a leisurely stroll along the quay. The vertical lines of the sailboat masts and the horizontal lines of the Veles e Vents building create interesting compositions for photography. If the weather is calm, you might even catch beautiful reflections on the water. The marina is always bustling with activity, from stand-up paddleboarding and surfing to children learning to sail in small boats.

↓ MARINA REAL JUAN CARLOS I

BREAKFAST, BRUNCH & COFFEE

DDL Boutique

Carrer de Sant Vicent Màrtir 52, 46002 Ciutat Vella, ddlboutique.com

A tempting display of sweet and savoury pastries with an Argentine twist. Choose from *empanadas* stuffed with ground beef, or tuna and tomato, or indulge in delicious *alfajores* filled with *dulce de leche*. The wide variety of pies and pastries makes it hard to resist sampling them all.

La Mas Bonita

Passeig Marítim de la Patacona 11, 46120 Alboraia, lamasbonita.es

The inviting turquoise and white decor of La Mas Bonita lives up to its name, as it's one of the most beautiful eateries. The atmospheric interior draws people in, but it's the delicious pies, refreshing smoothies, and hearty sandwiches that keep them coming back for more.

Eras Pan Tienda

Carrer de Guillem de Castro 57, 46008 Extramurs, eraspan.com

For those with a sweet tooth, Eras Pan Tienda is a true paradise. The doughnuts, cinnamon rolls, cookies, and XL chocolate croissants are irresistibly delicious, making this bakery a must-visit. You'll find yourself returning to try each treat.

Café ArtySana

Carrer de Dénia 49, 46004 L'Eixample, cafeartysana.com

Café ArtySana is a perfect spot for any time of day, though their brunches really shine. Whether you're in the mood for yoghurt with granola and fresh fruit or whole wheat toast topped with grilled cheese and veggies, this café offers a satisfying and welcoming experience.

Nuez Café

Carrer del Convent de Sant Francesc 6, 46002 Ciutat Vella, insta @nuezcafe

Just steps from the bustling Plaza Ayuntamiento, Nuez Café offers a peaceful retreat. Enjoy a hearty breakfast or brunch in this friendly bakery or take in the morning air at their outdoor terrace, perfect for starting the day right.

Eggcellent

Avinguda de l'Oest 33, 46001 Ciutat Vella, eggcellent.es

If your breakfast isn't complete without eggs, go to Eggcellent. Try *Los Benny de Salmón* or *Los Benny de Bacon*, delicious eggs Benedict with salmon or bacon. This all-day brunch spot is perfect for egg lovers looking for a satisfying meal.

Federal Café

Carrer de l'Ambaixador Vich 15, 46002 Ciutat Vella, federalcafe.es

Federal Café is a spacious and relaxing spot with a coworking vibe. The large shared tables in front are perfect for working or socialising, and the menu features items like pancakes, pastrami sandwiches, and iced vanilla lattes.

La Petite Brioche

Carrer de Sorní 28, 46004 L'Eixample, lapetitebrioche.es

The charming vintage bakery La Petite Brioche offers a variety of savoury and sweet treats alongside a tasty brunch menu. Each day, you can enjoy fresh and healthy options at an affordable price, making it a great place for a delightful meal.

Boscon Coffee

Carrer de Finlàndia 16, 46010 El Pla del Real, bosconcoffee.com

Boscon Coffee offers an extensive brunch menu with everything from smoothies and granola bowls to bagels, pancakes, and eggs. Their high-quality coffee is renowned in Valencia, making it a popular spot for coffee lovers and brunch enthusiasts alike.

Bluebell Coffee Co.

Carrer de Buenos Aires 3, 46006 L'Eixample, bluebellcoffeeco.com

They roast their own carefully selected coffee beans at Bluebell Coffee Co. The café features a lovely green courtyard and serves unique dishes, like waffles with pulled pork or chia pudding with mango, alongside their expertly brewed coffee.

Horchateria Santa Catalina

Plaça de Santa Caterina 6, 46001 Ciutat Vella, horchateriasantacatalina.com

The most iconic spot for trying *horchata* is Horchateria Santa Catalina. The traditional Valencian drink is made from tiger nuts, water, and sugar. Paired with a *farton* pastry, this sweet, refreshing drink makes for a perfect breakfast or snack.

Brunch Corner

Carrer del Comte d'Almodóvar 1, 46003 Ciutat Vella, brunchcorner.es

Brunch Corner is always bustling, but the wait is never too long. It's well worth it for the freshly squeezed orange juice, excellent coffee, and mouthwatering sandwiches that make this spot a local favourite.

PAELLA & OTHER RICE DISHES

La Tasqueta del Mercat

Carrer del Mestre Aguilar 2, 46006 L'Eixample, latasquetadelmercat.com

Next to the Mercado de Ruzafa, you'll find La Tasqueta del Mercat. The bar has a lunch menu at a reasonable price, with homemade focaccia, croquetas, paella, and artisanal ice cream. The welcoming, relaxed vibe is sure to lift your spirits.

El Bar Cremaet

Avinguda del Port 20, 46021 El Pla del Real, barcremaet.com

Good traditional Valencian food is served at El Bar Cremaet. This is not a touristy spot, but rather a modern, local place to enjoy a rice dish. Order a coffee Cremaet after your meal: it contains rum, sugar, spices, and lemon peel.

Restaurante Panorama

Carrer Marina Real Juan Carlos I, 46011 Poblados Maritimos, panoramarestaurante.com

Restaurante Panorama offers some of the most breathtaking beach views in Valencia. While Valencians typically enjoy their paella at lunchtime, stay a bit longer for a refreshing cocktail (or mocktail) as the sun sets over the city skyline and the beach.

Restaurante Navarro

Carrer de l'Arquebisbe Mayoral 5, 46002 Ciutat Vella, restaurantenavarro.com

Since 1951, Restaurante Navarro has been a Valencia staple, known for its fresh, healthy Mediterranean dishes. Their ingredients are sourced directly from the Central Market and Mercado Ruzafa, ensuring the highest quality. Don't miss out on one of their celebrated rice dishes!

TAPAS & STREET FOOD

Malvón

Passatge de Russafa 2, 46002 Ciutat Vella, malvon.es

Malvón is a street food bar where they serve typical Argentinian *empanadas*, savoury, filled pastries with ground beef, chicken, caprese, tuna, and much more. Some are spicy and others nice and cheesy. For dessert, choose their sweet raspberry chocolate bonbons or the traditional Alfajor de Maizena, melt-in-the-mouth biscuits. A quick and delicious takeaway.

100 Montaditos

spain.100montaditos.com

The 100 Montaditos restaurants are everywhere in the city. You can order several small bread rolls with more than one hundred different fillings to choose from. They also offer fries, chicken or cheese fingers, olives, and tacos. You order and pay at the counter, leave your name and collect your food after a few minutes. On Wednesdays and Sundays, they have a special deal, and you can order any sandwich from the menu for just €1.

Tanto Monta

Carrer del Poeta Artola 19, 46021 Algirós, insta @tanto_monta_vlc

Tapas bar Tanto Monta is based in the student district. You can choose from many delicious sandwiches in the display case, with a *tortilla de patata* (potato omelette), salmon, hamburger, cured ham, or melted goat's cheese with jam. Order the ones you love and add a drink. Take a seat on one of the bar stools or at the small tables in the back.

Bodega La Rentaora

Plaça de Mossén Sorell 11, 46003 Ciutat Vella, larentaora.com

The terrace of Bodega La Rentaora is a unique spot next to the Mercado de Mossen Sorrell in El Carmen. The tapas of this small restaurant are a delight. You must try the aubergine salad and the hummus or the *montaditos* (small sandwiches) with smoked sardines and grated tomato, or the serrano ham with brie.

Quesometero Cheesebar

Carrer del Mestre Clavé 8, 46001 Ciutat Vella, quesomentero.com

You will find over 120 different cheeses at cheese lover's paradise Quesometero Cheesebar. The special menu lets you taste a wide variety of different cheeses, and different preparations. Cheese is the main ingredient of all dishes and if you don't know what to order, just say cheese!

Sagardi

Carrer de Sant Vicent Màrtir 6, 46002 Ciutat Vella, sagardi.com

Sagardi is a Basque pintxos bar. Pintxos are small pieces of bread with a wooden skewer to keep toppings fixed to the bread. When you ask for the bill, the waiter will come to your table and count the skewers to see how many you ate to calculate the amount. Ask for the slightly sparkling, low-alcohol Basque white wine: Txacoli.

Pizzeria Raices

Carrer Bailía 2, 46003 Valencia, pizzeriaraices.es

This small cafeteria is known for their delicious Pizza Napolitana. And don't leave as soon as you've finished your pizza at Pizzeria Raices. Ask them for *postres* (desserts)! We love the *Babá con crema de Pistacho*.

Bodega la Peseta

Carrer del Crist del Grau 16, 46011 Poblats Marítims, insta @lapeseta_bodega

Until 2002, Spain's currency was the peseta. Bodega la Peseta is a typical Spanish bodega that opened their doors in 1906, and the interior still seems to be from that time. They have the best *tortilla de patata* in town. Also, ask them for the daily special, as they make a paella and *fideua* (a pasta dish) for their regulars.

La Chata Ultramarinos

Carrer del Literat Azorín 4, 46006 L'Eixample, lachataultramarinos.es

From the outside, La Chata Ultramarinos looks like a local supermarket from about a hundred years ago. Go in and take a seat on one of the small chairs at an even smaller table inside or on the terrace. You'll be surprised with the food: their tapas-sized foods are all prepared with lots of creativity.

Taberna La Sénia

Carrer de la Sénia 2, 46001 Ciutat Vella, tabernalasenia.es

Tapas bar Taberna La Sénia is a mix of Tuscan and Valencian traditions. They prioritise sustainability by sourcing fresh, local products from Valencian markets and using regionally certified items like Pastuenca beef. Their wine list features organic selections from small wineries. Since 2020, they've been growing seasonal vegetables and producing LOLIO Organic Extra Virgin Olive Oil, which is used in their cooking.

Bar Cabanyal

Carrer de Martí Grajales 5, 46011 Poblats Marítims

Do you like fish, shellfish, and crustaceans but don't want to spend a lot in an expensive restaurant? Bar Cabanyal is a simple bar with all the best produce directly from the market on the other side of the road. Order some gambas, pulpo, crab salad in a shell, coquilles, and small fish fritters.

FOOD MARKETS

Mercado de la Imprenta

Carrer de la Mascota 17, 46007 Extramurs, mercadodelaimprenta.com

This stylish, modern food market features 21 stalls offering dishes from Spain and beyond. Set in a former printing house, the market centres on an area with palm trees and a bar, perfect for dining or chatting with neighbours. This versatile space also hosts wine tastings, art classes, and pop-up markets, creating a vibrant, multi-purpose atmosphere.

Mercabañal

Carrer d'Eugènia Viñes 225, 46011 Poblats Marítims, mercabanyal.com

For a relaxed, beachy surfer vibe, head to Mercabañal. This casual open-air spot near the beach is perfect for unwinding after a seaside day, with food trucks offering tapas, burgers, bao buns, and ice cream. Spread across a ground floor and upper level, Mercabañal welcomes sandy feet and chill vibes as part of the experience.

Mercader

Carrer de Joan Mercader 16, 46011 Poblats Maritims, mercadercabanyal.com

At Mercader, you'll meet friends to enjoy some good tapas and a drink. The nine different stalls serve many small bites as well as full meals. This industrial venue was a workshop for coopers who made wooden barrels. Mercader was founded with a deep respect for tradition and craftsmanship, blending a natural sense of progress with timeless values.

Mercado de Colón

Carrer de Jorge Juan 19, 46004 L'Eixample, mercadocolon.es

Once a busy market for fresh produce, meat, and poultry, Mercado de Colón is now a vibrant food hall filled with restaurants and bars. Stop by Mi Cub for tapas, Down Monkey Business for a cocktail, or enjoy the terraces of Suc de Lluna Biocafé and Casa de L'Orxata, offering winter sun and summer shade.

DINNER

Tinto Fino Ultramarino

Carrer de la Corretgeria 38, 46001 Ciutat Vella, insta @tintofinoultramarino

In a nice little street in the historic city centre, you'll find Tinto Fino Ultramarino, a tapas bar where you can enjoy good tapas and good wine. Their slogan is *ahorra agua, bebe vino* ('save water, drink wine'). The Mediterranean dishes have Spanish as well as Italian influences, and their favourite dishes are the cannelloni filled with *rabo de toro* (oxtail) and bechamel, or the angus meatballs with tomato sauce.

Saona

gruposaona.com

A small chain of restaurants in Valencia and the surrounding area where they serve a reasonably priced menu for lunch and dinner. There is a good selection of dishes, so everyone can pick their favourite, with good vegetarian options as well. You can find them in some of the best locations around town. Their interior has a nice and calm beachy atmosphere.

Maui Russafa

Carrer dels Vivons 27, 46006 L'Eixample, mauirussafa.com

This restaurant offers unpretentious, freshly prepared meals featuring chicken, mushrooms, cheese, and vegetables. The lively decor at Maui Russafa, with plants and bookshelves, makes you feel like you're in a welcoming living room. This pet-friendly spot warmly welcomes well-behaved dogs and cats, creating a comfortable, homely atmosphere.

La Finestra

Carrer dels Vivons 16, 46006 L'Eixample, insta @lafinestraruzafa

No reservations can be made at La Finestra, so arrive early. These are the town's best, most affordable pizzas, at just €2.80 for small ones. Two rules apply: order as many pizzas as you like in one go, and let the chef pick the ingredients (while considering dietary restrictions).

Somos Raro Restaurante

Passatge de l'Albereda 10, 46010 El Pla del Real, somosrarorestaurante.com

Somos Raro means 'we are strange', and perhaps they are at this restaurant, but they have a good chef preparing delicious meals. You can choose a menu that they call *para no pensar* ('not to think') with five or six savoury dishes and one

dessert to share. Or you can order *la normalidad es insoportable* ('normality is unbearable') from the menu.

Latte & Farina

Plaça Redona 1, 46001 Ciutat Vella, latteefarina.es

At the beautiful round Plaza Redonda, with its fountain and artisan shops selling ceramics, lace, and embroidery, you'll also find Latte & Farina. This ultimate Italian restaurant prepares pasta in a parmesan cheese at your table. The pizza with pistachio pesto and mortadella is a delight. And for dessert, try the *pizza speciale Ferrero Rocher*.

Damura Ramen

Carrer del Doctor Serrano 17, 46006 L'Eixample, damuraramen.com

Blending Chinese and Japanese culinary traditions inspired by Chinese immigrants in Japan, Damura Ramen offers a unique dining experience. Valencia's first ramen bar offers artisanal dishes like ramen, bao buns, and hane gyoza. Its vibrant, global-inspired space features slow-cooked broths and ingredients from Mexico, Korea, and beyond, transforming street food into a great dining experience.

Mamma Pazzo

Carrer del Comte de Salvatierra 37, 46004 L'Eixample, mammapazzo.es

It is all about the experience at Mamma Pazzo. This American-style Italian restaurant makes dining out exciting and fun. Cocktails come in cups shaped like Diego Maradona, Al Pacino, and Michelangelo's David. With a hidden area behind the library, red velvet curtains, stylish plates, and unique oil-and-vinegar sets, the ambience adds flair to the delicious food.

Éter

Carrer d'Antoni Suárez 31, 46021 El Pla del Real, etervalencia.com

Éter is a Mediterranean restaurant with Korean influences. The steak tartare is served on a *farton* (traditional sweet pastry), they have a mini brioche with *rabo de toro* (oxtail), and the salad with burrata, grilled aubergine, and escarole is delicious. You can also enjoy a Korean BBQ. Don't leave the restaurant before you try one of their signature cocktails.

La Diva

Carrer de Sorni 42, 46004 L'Eixample, ladivavalencia.com

As soon as you enter the restaurant and club La Diva, you'll be amazed. Large LED displays on the walls and ceiling continuously show sceneries of tropical beaches or rainforest waterfalls. The Art Deco interior reminds you of a roaring twenties party with jazzy music and Charleston dancers. The quality of the food is excellent, given its price.

Begin

Carrer de Pascual i Genís 11, 46002 Ciutat Vella, beginrestaurante.com

Begin is referring to where it all began, back to basic, back to nature. Begin sources plant-based ingredients primarily from local farmers near each restaurant. When local sourcing isn't possible, they prioritise national suppliers committed to environmental balance. Quality is key, as is close collaboration with farmers, to connect communities with the best produce. All non-plant proteins align with OIE Animal Welfare standards, ensuring free-range, grass-fed standards.

Zazu

Avinguda de les Corts Valencianes 22, 46015 Benicalap, zazulounge.com

Zazu offers a dining experience set in a lush tropical forest, with vibrant birds watching from above. The menu features a variety of dishes, including burgers, salads, sushi, and poke bowls. With its stylish yet relaxed atmosphere, warm hospitality, and well-priced menus, it's an ideal spot to celebrate birthdays and have gatherings with friends.

Estación Cero

Carrer de Cadis 47, 46004 L'Eixample, insta @estacioncero_valencia

In Ruzafa, you'll find a small Argentinian spot called Estación Cero. Even for Argentinians this is the place to eat *empanadas con salsa chimichurri* (savoury pastries with a sauce of fresh herbs, oil, and vinegar), sandwiches with Argentinian beef, melted cheese with chorizo, and burgers. Their soul food is a real treat on any occasion.

La Ofrenda

Avinguda de França 36, 46023 Camins al Grau, laofrendagourmet.com

At La Ofrenda, you'll taste authentic Mexican tacos and quesadillas. They came to

Valencia eagerly wanting to share Mexico's rich culture. Their aim is to create an unforgettable experience, transporting guests to vibrant Mexico and leaving great memories that bring joy to life's most special moments. On Fridays, there is live music, cocktails are all masterpieces, and the whole environment is colourful and vibrant.

Madre

Carrer d'Eugènia Viñes 227, 46011 Poblats Marítims, lawebdemadre.com

Near the beach, Latin restaurant Madre invites you to savour soulful dishes any time of day, offering a warm and welcoming atmosphere. Enjoy fresh, laid-back Latin-inspired cuisine in the charming green patio with cactuses and banana plants, or in their cosy cantina. Try the Peruvian ceviche or fries with *mojo verde* (sauce of green jalapeño, avocado, coriander, and lime zest).

Hundred Burgers

Carrer de Sant Vicent Màrtir 44, 46001 Ciutat Vella, hundredburgers.com

Alex and Eze started Hundred Burgers as their own challenge in 2017. They really loved burgers, bought a ticket to New York and tried fifteen of the best burgers in town in just four days. Since then, their team travelled over 22 countries and tasted more than 300 burgers to prepare their own perfect burgers. In 2024 they won the World's Best Burgers award, the equivalent to a Michelin star in the burger community.

Voltereta Bali

Gran Via del Marqués del Túria 59, 46005 L'Eixample, volteretarestaurante.com

Voltereta Bali is one of four unique Voltereta restaurants in Valencia, each offering a distinct experience. Stepping inside feels like teleporting to another world, in this case, the vibrant markets of Indonesia. Bali's menu features tapas-style dishes

blending Asian and Spanish flavours, perfect for sharing, such as *nasi goreng* (Balinese fried rice with vegetables and chicken), *bao Hoisin* (bao bread filled with pork), and Korean ribs.

BRING THE PARENTS

Bouet

Gran Via de les Germanies 34, 46006 Ensanche, bouetrestaurant.es

Bouet blends Mediterranean and cosmopolitan flavours with art, music, and design. The passionate young team creates fresh and ethical dishes. Would you like to try oysters, duck, and chive dumplings, steak or tuna tartare, or chicken satay? Each dish is as beautifully presented as the next. This restaurant is perfect for a celebration.

Dos Estaciones

Carrer del Pintor Salvador Abril 28, 46005 L'Eixample, restaurante2estaciones.com

Mar Soler and Alberto Alonso are the two faces of Dos Estaciones ('two seasons'). They focus on seasonal cuisine as its core philosophy. Each season brings transformation and evolution, reflecting their belief that to change the world, one must first transform their product. You can also order a tasting menu, letting the chef surprise you.

Vaqueta Gastro Mercat

Carrer de Sant Ferran 22, 46001 Ciutat Vella, grupogastrotrinquet.com

Located next to the Central Market, Vaqueta Gastro Mercat offers dishes made with ingredients sourced directly from that market. The modern interior includes private dining areas and an open space for savouring crispy artichokes, grilled cuttlefish, red tuna tartare, sushi, sashimi, and Valencian rice dishes.

COCKTAIL BARS & ROOFTOPS

Atenea Sky

Carrer de Moratín 12, 46002 Ciutat Vella, ateneasky.com

Rooftop bar Atenea Sky is a fantastic venue to look over the rooftops of the historic city centre, with the best view of Plaza Ayuntamiento and its town hall. The sky bar has over 400 square metres of outdoor space to enjoy a cocktail and some bites, while listening to a live DJ. You can also make a reservation for lunch or dinner in one of their dedicated spaces.

Gran Martínez

Avinguda del Port 318, 46024 Poblados Marítmos, insta @gran_martinez

Gran Martínez is housed in a former pharmacy with wood panelling on the walls and ceilings. Now it is a mysterious-looking vintage cocktail bar, with dimmed, indirect lights, and curtains leading into various sections. There are many intimate spots where you can take a seat for a classic vermouth with an olive and a plate of cured ham.

The Jungle

Carrer del Comte d'Altea 12, 46005 L'Eixample, thejunglevalencia.es

Welcome to The Jungle. The drinks are the true gems here, with names like Blue Frog, Wild Tiger, and Mad Monkey. The exotic and vibrant atmosphere complements the exclusive drinks and their delicious tapas menu.

Café de Madrid

Carrer de l'Abadia de Sant Martí 10, 46002 Ciutat Vella, insta @cafemadridvalencia

This bar is where the famous cocktail Agua de Valencia (cava, orange juice, vodka, and gin) originated. It reopened recently as part of the hotel Marques House. In the early 20th century, Café de Madrid was a renowned literary café, drawing visitors from across Spain. Its walls now display images from that era, capturing the spirit of a time when the Valencian bourgeoisie gathered here.

Apotheke

Carrer de Ciscar 18, 46005 L'Eixample, apothekevlc.com

This is Valencia's first speakeasy, inspired by the hidden bars of the U.S. Prohibition Era (1920-1933), when alcohol was covertly served. Since the early 2000s, this trend of concealing cocktail bars behind unassuming names or discreet entrances, like Apotheke, has gained popularity.

Café de las Horas

Carrer del Comte d'Almodóvar 1, 46003 Ciutat Vella, cafedelashoras.com

Café de las Horas has become the go-to spot for its renowned Agua de Valencia, a cocktail crafted with freshly pressed orange juice and their signature liqueur. The bar's baroque ambiance transports you to another era, with lavish mirrors, marble accents, vibrant colours, chandeliers, and abundant flowers and oranges. You'd expect Marie Antoinette herself to walk through the door at any moment.

Palacio Santa Clara

Carrer de Pascual i Genís 22, 46002 Ciutat Vella, insta @palaciosantaclara

In 1916, the Valencian architect Francisco Javier Goerlich completed the Niederleytner family residence, a modernist Art Deco building that now serves as the Palacio Santa Clara hotel. The design embraces a fresh, organic style influenced by nature, with rounded shapes, flowing curves, and exotic motifs. But the true highlight is its chill-out rooftop bar, where you can relax with stunning views over the city.

Maison Lupin

Carrer de l'Almirall Cadarso 12, 46005 L'Eixample, maisonlupin.es

Why sip your cocktail from an ordinary glass when at Maison Lupin you can enjoy it from character cups? Try a piña colada served in a Tintin cup, a refined classic in a Sherlock Holmes mug, or a gin-based cocktail inspired by Queen Elizabeth. With dim lighting, velvet curtains, and laid-back live music on weekends, it's the perfect spot for an after-dinner drink.

↓ CAFÉ DE LAS HORAS

↓ FABRICA DE HIELO

PUBS & WINE BARS

Café Negrito

Plaça del Negret 1, 46001 Ciutat Vella, insta @cafenegritovalencia

In Valencia's El Carmen neighbourhood you'll find Bar Negrito, a favourite for its relaxed vibe and classic tapas. Located in Plaça del Negrito, it is perfect for people-watching and enjoying the bustling energy of the square. With a solid selection of wines, beers, and tapas, it's an ideal spot for a casual night out.

Café Berlin

Carrer de Cadis 22-24, 46006 L'Eixample, cafeberlinvalencia.es

There is always something happening at Café Berlin. The bar is famous for its language exchange nights. On Mondays it's French vs Spanish, Tuesdays are for Japanese and Spanish, and Wednesdays for English and Spanish – or just come along and have a good time. On other days, you can expect cocktail workshops and exhibitions. Overall, the bar has a *buen rollo*, a nice vibe.

Bodega Filà El Labrador

Carrer del Dr. Manuel Candela 58, 46021 Algirós

Looking for a very traditional local wine bar? Visit Bodega Filà El Labrador. Don't expect a fancy place, just enjoy the neighbours stopping by for a drink, a bite, and a chat with the waiter. But don't be fooled by the outdated interior; the best local wines are served at

a very reasonable price. Order some olives, ham, cheese, and chorizo with your wine served straight from the barrel.

St. Patrick's

Gran Via del Marqués del Túria 69, 46005 L'Eixample, stpatricksvalencia.com

St. Patrick's is an authentic Irish bar. Check their website for live music, language exchanges, meetups, trivia, bingo, and beer pong nights. Many matches are broadcast live, like football, NBA, boxing, darts, F1, and MotoGP. Happy hour takes place every Friday between 4 pm and 7 pm.

Vive Vino Natural Wine Bar

Carrer del Pintor Salvador Abril 13, 46005 L'Eixample, insta @vivevino_winebar

Run by Marta and Nieves, Vive Vino Natural Wine Bar specialises in natural, ancestral, and orange wines, offering a fantastic selection by the glass, bottle, or to take home. Enjoy artisanal cheese boards, charcuterie, gourmet preserves, and delicious pastrami and porchetta sandwiches in a relaxed, welcoming atmosphere curated with passion and expertise.

Cuatro Monos

Carrer de la Reina Na Maria 7, 46004 L'Eixample, insta @cuatromonosvalencia

The lively bar Cuatro Monos in the bustling Ruzafa neighbourhood is known for its cold beer, great music, and friendly atmosphere. The food is tasty, perfect for a mid-drink snack and the quality cocktails make it ideal for a relaxed night out with friends or your partner. Altogether, it's the perfect cocktail for a great evening.

Parabarap

Carrer de Polo y Peyrolón 11, 46021 El Pla del Real, insta @parabarapvalencia

Student bar Parabarap is in Valencia's university area, popular for its relaxed vibe and affordable drinks. Known for their student-friendly prices and frequent happy hours, it attracts both local and international students. With occasional themed nights, live DJ sets, and a welcoming atmosphere, it's an ideal spot to unwind, socialise, and enjoy a fun night out.

La Boba y el Gato Rancio

Carrer de Cuba 59, 46006 L'Eixample, insta @labobayelgatorancio

You can find this quirky, vintage queer-friendly bar with laid-back vibe in Valencia's Ruzafa district. Popular for its creative cocktails, craft beers, and unique tapas, La Boba y el Gato Rancio ('the fool and the rancid cat') features mismatched furniture and nostalgic, eclectic decor. It's a favourite among locals and visitors seeking a relaxed, artsy atmosphere with an offbeat charm.

LIVE MUSIC

Fabrica de Hielo

Carrer de Pavia 37, 46011 Poblats Marítims, lafabricadehielo.net

The former ice factory Fabrica de Hielo stands next to the sea and in its day produced ice to keep newly caught fish fresh. This place is now one of the coolest cultural venues. The industrial open space is perfect for small concerts and exhibitions.

The Artist Bar

Carrer de Bello 3, 46024 Poblats Marítims, insta @theartistvalencia

A little bar in the port area. The Artist Bar is popular among students from Berklee College of Music in Valencia. The owner organises small gigs and a talent show. Not a crowded place, just an out-of-the-way spot to have a drink and listen to some music.

Radio City

Carrer de Santa Teresa 19, 46001 Ciutat Vella, radiocityvalencia.es

Radio City is well-known in town for its flamenco performances, midweek reggae, and Sunday funk jam sessions. It is one of those places where you can go seven days a week to party and find others that want to have a fun time. Depending on the night and performances, you can experience completely different vibes every time.

Jimmy Glass Jazz Bar

Carrer de Baix 28, 46003 Ciutat Vella, jimmyglassjazz.net

Jimmy Glass Jazz Bar is often packed with jazz fanatics. Recognised internationally, including by *DownBeat Magazine* as one of the world's best jazz clubs in 2018, Jimmy Glass is known for its cosmopolitan vibe and dedication to quality music. The venue frequently offers a diverse lineup of concerts, making it a cultural hotspot in Valencia.

Black Note Club

Carrer de Polo y Peyrolón 15, 46021 El Pla del Real, blacknoteclub.com

The live music hotspot Black Note Club has been open since 1993, hosting over 6,000 concerts. Specialising in rock, R&B, funk, and more, it blends excellent acoustics with emerging talent. Open Wednesdays to Saturdays, it's a cultural beacon with vibrant performances and community events.

Loco Club

Carrer de l'Erudit Orellana 12, 46008 Extramurs, lococlub.es

With a capacity of 300, Loco Club offers the perfect size for intimate concerts. The music performances offer a wide range from country, indie, pop, soul, to punk and rock 'n' roll. There are two bars and there is a small, seated area where you can enjoy your night out to the max.

Peter Rock Club

Carrer de Quart 26, 46001 Ciutat Vella, peterrockclub.es

In Valencia's Barrio del Carmen, you'll find Peter Rock Club, a prominent live music venue known for its diverse programming. It features rock, blues, and swing performances from national and international artists. The venue also hosts DJ sessions, photography exhibitions, and family-friendly events. Its central location attracts both locals and tourists.

La Vitti

Plaça del Xúquer 3, 46021 Algirós, insta @lavittibar

The cultural bar La Vitti in Valencia's Plaça del Xúquer is a haven for live music, art, and creative gatherings. Founded with a passion for music, it offers events like jazz nights, jam sessions, and innovative experiences such as Discohike (live music during a hike in the surrounding mountains). Its owners, tied by shared artistic visions, keep the venue vibrant.

Café del Duende

Carrer del Túria 62, 46008 Extramurs, cafedelduende.com

Established in 1998, Café del Duende was Valencia's premier venue for authentic flamenco. Located near the Torres de Quart, it showcases professional performances in an intimate setting Thursdays to Sundays. Shows last an hour, and reservations or online ticket sales are not available. Early arrival is recommended.

Matisse Club

Carrer de Campoamor 60, 46022 Algirós, matisseclub.com

Matisse Club is a vibrant venue in the student district known for its diverse live music offerings. The club organises weekly Wednesday flamenco shows, hosts jam sessions on Thursdays, and every Sunday is for jazz and easy listening.

CLUBS

Marina Beach Club

Calle Marina Real Juan Carlos I, 46011 Poblados Marítimos, marinabeachclub.com

Palm trees, sunbeds, beach umbrellas, a swimming pool, delicious food, and unmatched views of the beach: Marina Beach Club. During the day, it's a relaxed spot to soak up the sun and enjoy a refreshing cocktail. From 4pm onwards, a DJ takes over, and the vibe shifts as the party intensifies throughout the night, continuing until 4am. Check the website for upcoming theme nights.

Club Mya & Umbracle

Avinguda del Professor López Piñero 5, 46013 Quatre Carreres, umbracleterraza.com

Club Mya and Umbracle are both located in the stunning City of Arts & Sciences. Club Mya is the indoor section of the venue, featuring two halls, each with distinct music and DJs. Umbracle is the outdoor area, set beneath arches and surrounded by a palm tree garden. It offers a dance floor, multiple bars, and VIP seats.

Akuarela Platja

Carrer d'Eugènia Viñes 152, 46011 Poblats Marítims, akuarelaplaya.es

Just a few steps from the beach, you'll find Akuarela Platja, offering stunning views of the Mediterranean. The venue combines comfortable lounge areas, stylish outdoor seating, and expansive spaces. It's renowned for its popular *tardeos* (early evening parties), which kick off at 5pm and run until midnight, as well as its famous Paris Nights events.

Fox Congo

Carrer dels Cavallers 35, 46001 Ciutat Vella, insta @foxcongo

Fox Congo is an atmospheric club in the heart of Valencia with a marble bar and graffiti. The DJ plays a wide range of electronic music, reggaeton, commercial hits, and everything in between. A popular spot for those looking to dance late into the night.

La3

Avinguda de Blasco Ibáñez 111, 46022 Algirós, la3club.com

To find the alternative electronic music scene in Valencia, go to La3 nightclub. It features a variety of DJ performances, ranging from techno and house to experimental and bass music. Known for its raw, industrial vibe, La3 offers an intimate atmosphere with cutting-edge sound systems and an energetic crowd.

Mini Club

Avinguda de Blasco Ibáñez 111, 46022 Algirós, insta @miniclub_valencia

The intimate, underground nightclub Mini Club offers a great nightlife experience. They focus on electronic music, particularly techno and house. Its underground vibe makes it perfect for an authentic, non-commercial clubbing experience in the city.

Play Club

Carrer de Cuba 8, 46004 L'Eixample, insta @playclubvlc

Play Club is in the trendy Ruzafa neighbourhood. It boasts two rooms: one playing electronic, indie, and urban music that draws a more alternative crowd, and the other dedicated to pop hits, rock, and classic rhythms for those with more traditional tastes.

Discoteca Indiana

Carrer de Sant Vicent Màrtir 95, 46004 Extramurs, discotecaindiana.com

The popular nightclub Discoteca Indiana is known for its lively atmosphere and diverse music, including mainstream hits, reggaeton, Latin rhythms, and EDM. It attracts a young crowd looking for a fun night out. The club opens around midnight until 5 or 6am.

Rumbo 144

Avinguda de Blasco Ibáñez 144, 46022 Algirós, insta @rumbo144oficial

Exchange students from the nearby university love Rumbo 144. The club hosts Latin nights, reggaeton parties, and special DJ sessions throughout the week. They also often host feature guest DJs and live performances.

QUEER

The Muse

Carrer de Ruaya 48, 46009 La Saïdia, insta @the_muse_valencia

The popular gay bar and nightclub The Muse can be found in trendy Ruzafa. Known for its vibrant, inclusive queer vibe, it attracts a stylish crowd who enjoy commercial hits, house, and EDM. There arethemed nights, guest DJs, and performances, offering a fun environment for the LGBTQ+ community and allies alike.

Deseo 54

Carrer de Pepita 13-15, 46009 La Saïdia, deseo54.com

Nights with drag shows and themed parties like Lady Gaga Night and Kylie Minogue Party are the best at Deseo 54. The club celebrates LGBTQ+ pride with special events during Valencia Pride in June.

Barberbirborbur

Carrer de Mossèn Femenia 15, 46004 L'Eixample, insta @barberclub_vlc

A mix of locals, tourists, and LGBTQ+ patrons is attracted to Barberbirborbur, offering an inclusive, open-minded environment. It's popular with young professionals, creatives, and students, making it a great spot to meet new people or enjoy a night out with friends. The vibe is laid-back yet vibrant, with an eclectic, artistic style.

HOW TO DRESS LIKE A LOCAL

If you want to blend in with the locals, there is no need to change your style too much. Valencians are accustomed to hot weather and prefer light, comfortable clothes during summer. Wearing bikinis and going shirtless is strictly reserved for the beach and swimming pools. Trees in the local parks provide much-needed shade, and locals go there to avoid direct sunlight in the hottest months. Sunbathers are almost always tourists.

Even if it's still 18 degrees, winter coats, scarves, hats, and gloves make their appearance from early October. And warm clothes are worn until late May, no matter the weather.

For special occasions, Valencians like to dress up or even wear traditional outfits. And you might want to join in for Las Fallas. For the festivities, women (*falleras*) dress in colourful floral-patterned dresses, matching shoes, lace aprons, and silver or gold jewellery. Men (*falleros*) wear shorts, knee socks, floral-patterned vests, and headscarves.

When it's time to party, Valencians dress to impress. On nights out, both women and men tend to dress up. For weddings, guests also dress to the nines, so avoid wearing a casual summer dress or jeans if you're invited to a wedding, as you may feel underdressed all day (and night).

FLEA MARKETS, VINTAGE & SECOND-HAND

El Rastro

Carrer de la Serradora, 46011 Beteró

El Rastro is the biggest flea market of Valencia, in the Betero neighbourhood. It starts early on Sunday mornings and for the best finds, you'd better be there soon after it opens. The flea market used to be held next to the Mestalla football stadium but has since moved to a new, dedicated space with facilities such as fences, rubbish bins, sockets, and benches. It is better organised than ever, and a Sunday morning well spent.

Street markets

All around town you can find street markets. These markets sell clothes, shoes, underwear, socks, second-hand items, plants, ceramics, wooden toys, handmade bags, and much more for low prices. If you love searching in big piles, you can find the most unique items. You will find a street market on any weekday: Mondays in Ruzafa, Tuesdays in Bailèn, Wednesdays in Avenida del Cid, Thursdays in Cabanyal, and Fridays in Benimaclet.

Flamingos Vintage Kilo

Carrer de Cadis 17, 46006 L'Eixample, flamingosvintagekilo.com

The trendy second-hand shop Flamingos Vintage Kilo specialises in vintage clothes sold by weight, offering a sustainable shopping experience. Their headquarters are in Texas, but most of their twenty-five shops are in Spanish

FLEA MARKETS, VINTAGE & SECOND-HAND

cities, with two in Valencia. Most special are their upcycled garments, for which they use vintage items to create extraordinary and unique new pieces that you won't find anywhere else.

El Monstruo

Carrer de Calatrava 11, 46001 Ciutat Vella, monstruoshop.com

The shop El Monstruo stocks unique retro pieces ranging from 1980s and 1990s fashion to classic styles from previous decades. Located in the El Carmen neighbourhood, it attracts a mix of fashion enthusiasts and those looking for one-of-a-kind items. El Monstruo focuses on sustainability, offering upcycled clothes and promoting eco-friendly shopping. This little shop is a treasure trove of fashionable quality pieces with a nostalgic twist.

Lavespa Roja

Carrer de la Bosseria 6, 46001 Ciutat Vella, insta @lavespa_roja

Lavespa Roja is a charming vintage shop known for its carefully curated collection of retro and vintage garments. Here, you'll find pieces from past decades, offering everything from classic 70s, 80s, and 90s fashion to more timeless, stylish items. With a special selection and a welcoming vibe, Lavespa Roja attracts fashion lovers seeking distinctive, high-quality vintage pieces.

SoHo del Carmen

Carrer dels Drets 33, 46001 Ciutat Vella, insta @sohodelcarmen

Looking for a leather or denim jacket? At SoHo del Carmen, you'll find styles to suit your taste. Their extensive selection of jeans is also impressive. If you're after a wardrobe essential, this shop is the place to go. So, reuse those beautiful boots and recycle that blouse, contributing to zero waste and a more sustainable environment.

Koopera Store

koopera.org

With five locations across Valencia, Koopera Store is a top destination for vintage shopping. In partnership with Caritas, Koopera helps integrate individuals at risk of social exclusion by offering them job opportunities in their shops. They collect textiles in large bins placed throughout the city, sort them, and either distribute them to those in need or sell them in their shops, supporting both sustainability and social inclusion.

Reborn Vintage Atelier

Carrer de Mossèn Femenia 20, 46006 L'Eixample, insta @rebornvintagevlc

Reborn Vintage Atelier offers colourful vintage pieces. The true magic happens in their workshop, where they upcycle ordinary garments into one-of-a-kind, fresh creations. They also provide repair services for your well-worn jeans or favourite coat, giving them a new lease of life. In addition, the shop features hand-painted art garments by Pablo Kalafaker, adding a unique artistic touch to their collection.

Aieclé Vintage

insta @aiecle_lale_vintage

This is a typical vintage 90s shop. Looking for a colourful disco-era tracksuit in pink, yellow, and light blue? You might find it at Aieclé Vintage. Don't leave before you have seen their embroidered denim jackets, Hawaii shirts, and old-school boots. They have opened another two shops, Aieclé Vintage 2 and Lale by Aieclé, also in the Ruzafa neighbourhood.

Reused.es (Reusado Vintage)

Carrer de Dénia 12, 46006 L'Eixample,
insta @reused.es

The place to find unique trainers is Reused.es (Reusado Vintage), which offers retro Jordans and Nike Dunk Highs and Lows. Their second-hand footwear is in excellent condition, with some pairs being true collector's items. The T-shirts available are unlike anything you've ever seen, and they sell Moncler. In addition to being a standout vintage shop, this spot also serves as a trendy barbershop and tattoo studio, making it a one-stop shop for style and creativity.

Vintaker

vintaker.com

At Vintaker you will find the best selection of vintage apparel from brands such as Nike, Adidas, Reebok, Lee, Fila, Ellesse, Guess, GAP, Levi's, Burberry, Ralph Lauren, Calvin Klein, Tommy, and Lacoste. And besides that, they stock beautifully vibrant shirts, jumpers, and dresses in their two shops in El Carmen and Ruzafa.

Mon Petit Secret

Plaça del Mercat 12, 46001 Ciutat Vella,
mon-petit-secret.com

You'll discover second-hand designer bags, belts, and watches at affordable prices at Mon Petit Secret. Their collection of sparkling brooches, necklaces, and earrings proves that glamour doesn't have to come with a hefty price tag. The shop also offers a selection of classy jackets and luxurious cashmere scarves. You'll find pieces from renowned brands such as Valentino, Loewe, Seiko, Dior, Gucci, Maurice Lacroix, and Swarovski, among others.

LAKA - Cultural artifacts & Vintage memorabilia

Carrer de Cadis 15, 46004 L'Eixample, lakafamily.com

LAKA - Cultural artifacts & Vintage memorabilia is a vintage shop that celebrates the art in clothing, objects, and what they describe as 'random stuff'. The clothing selection includes everything from T-shirts and velvet jackets to iconic football tops and caps. As for the 'random stuff', expect to find a diverse range of items like vases, lighters, miniature cars, chairs, radios, vintage magazines, and retro alarm clocks, each with a unique story of its own.

3 Coolcats Vintage & Retro

Carrer del Músic Peydró 28, 46001 Ciutat Vella, 3coolcats.es

Ilana and Emilio from 3 Coolcats Vintage & Retro are experts in vintage clothes and Mid-century furniture. Ilana, with a background in fashion design and visual merchandising for luxury brands, has spent nearly twenty years buying and selling vintage. Emilio, passionate about Mid-century decor, also specialises in vintage clothes and has an eye for hidden gems. Together, they bring their shared passion to their shops in Lisbon and Valencia.

La Chase Retro & Med

Carrer del Mestre Clavé 3, 46001 Ciutat Vella, insta @lachaiseretroandmed

La Chase Retro & Med is a unique concept store blending casual fashion, art, and design. It is a source of inspiration for creative minds, featuring a vibrant mix of upcycled dresses, bags, colourful floral shirts, shoes, and jewellery. It is all designed by innovative artists. On Thursdays, the team collects old items and furniture from the streets, restoring them and breathing new life into them.

STREETWEAR

Grimey Store

Carrer de Cadis 38, 46006 L'Eixample, grimey.com

Apparel, accessories, and limited-edition pieces, Grimey Store is a go-to destination for fashion-forward, edgy fashion enthusiasts.

Nude Project

Carrer de Martínez Ferrando 1, 46004 L'Eixample, nude-project.com

Nude Project is a stylish concept store offering contemporary streetwear with an artistic twist. Known for its unique designs, bold graphics, and high-quality materials, it's a favourite among fashion-forward locals.

PSTR Store

Avinguda de Blasco Ibáñez 33, 46010 El Pla del Real, wearestrap.com

The cutting-edge streetwear shop Strap offers trendy trainers and minimalist clothes with a bold urban aesthetic. Known for its exclusive collections and vibrant designs, it's a popular destination for modern, stylish shoppers.

Skateworld SW Best Brands

Carrer de la Pau 11, 46003 Ciutat Vella, skateworld.es

A top destination for skateboarders, offering a wide range of boards, accessories, and apparel from leading brands. They are known for quality, expert advice, and their streetwear.

Studio Store VLC

Gran Via del Marqués del Túria 18, 46005 L'Eixample, studiostorevlc.com

If you are looking for street-chic fashion, Studio Store VLC is your place. You will find bold urban brands like Dickies, Carrer, Noir, House of Sunny, Goodies Sportive, and Palard. The fashion-forward sporty look of most items strikes a balance between edgy and sophisticated.

Legit Sneaker House

Plaça de l'Ajuntament 23, 46002 Ciutat Vella,
legitsneakerhouse.com

Legit Sneaker House is one of the most diverse sneaker shops in the city. You will find retro trainers, playful shoes with bold prints, special editions from well-known brands, and accessories.

Gondwana Surf Valencia

Gran Via de les Germanies 25, 46006 Ensanche,
gondwanasurf.com

Being a city so close to the Mediterranean Sea, Gondwana Surf Valencia provides all you need to look fierce on the beach. Besides contemporary streetwear, you will find cool gadgets and essentials when you want to go surfing, paddle surfing or surf skating.

GOT'EM VLC

Carrer de Bonaire 13, 46002 Ciutat Vella,
gotemvlc.com

The small store GOT'EM VLC has an exclusive collection of limited-edition trainers, caps, T-shirts, and jumpers. Catering to sneakerheads and fashion enthusiasts, the shop stocks sought-after brands and rare releases, creating a must-visit location for those looking to elevate their street style.

Kaotiko

Carrer del Comte de Salvatierra 29, 46004 L'Eixample,
kaotikobcn.com

Founded in 1999 in Barcelona, Kaotiko promotes local, sustainable fashion with a commitment to quality and ethical production. The brand prioritises responsible consumption, fair working conditions, and eco-friendly materials. It aims to reduce environmental impact while offering exclusive, high-quality garments.

DEPARTMENT STORES

El Corte Inglés

elcorteingles.es

Spain's largest department store chain is called El Corte Inglés and can be found in several locations in Valencia. On Carrer de Colón, you'll find two eight-storey buildings, one dedicated to fashion and the other to electronics, books, and furniture. Close to the City of Arts and Sciences, there's the Agua Multiespacio shopping centre, which also houses El Corte Inglés. Another location can be found at Nuevo Centro shopping mall, next to the Túria metro station. El Corte Inglés offers a wide range of famous brands across various categories.

Mercat de Tapineria

Carrer de la Tapineria 15, 46001 Ciutat Vella, mercadodetapineria.com

This is a cultural and creative space in the heart of Valencia. Mercat de Tapineria is a hub for local artists, designers, and entrepreneurs, and hosts various pop-up shops, artisan markets, and events. At Mercat de Tapineria, you can find a mix of fashion, art, crafts, and food, where you can experience the city's creative scene and find unique, handmade products.

FNAC

Carrer de Guillem de Castro 9-11, 46007 Extramurs

The major French retail chain FNAC offers a wide range of products, including electronics, books, music, films, and video games. You can find FNAC on one of Valencia's main shopping streets.

Coolgifts Store

Carrer de Ciril Amorós 24, 46004 L'Eixample, coolgifts.store

Coolgifts Store is a fun and quirky shop offering unique gifts, gadgets, and accessories. Specialising in novelty items, personalised gifts, and creative home decor, it's the perfect spot for finding original and playful products that add a touch of fun to everyday life.

Passatge de Ripalda

Passatge de Ripalda

This quaint pedestrian passageway is home to an array of independent shops, cafés, and art galleries, and is a unique, hidden gem. One shop that stands out is Siente Valencia, which offers a selection of typical Valencian products, such as rice liqueur, spicy sausages, and fireworks-shaped chocolates.

Plaza Redonda

Plaza Redonda

If you're looking for artisanal shops offering ceramics, jewellery, lace, and pottery, you should visit Plaza Redonda. The central fountain is a popular spot where you can often see local artisans making lace. Around the fountain, small shops sell handcrafted treasures.

↓ LA POSTALERA

BOOKSHOPS

Librería Patagonia

Carrer del Hospital 1,
46001 Ciutat Vella,
libreriapatagonia.com

Librería Patagonia has been around since 1998 and sells adventurous travel books. Specialising in mountain expeditions, they also sell accessories that you need on your travels, such as backpacks, water bottles, maps, and travel notebooks.

El Doctor Sax –
Beat & Books

Carrer de Quart 21,
46001 Ciutat Vella,
insta @eldoctorsax

The artistic bookshop and publisher El Doctor Sax – Beat & Books offers books in Spanish, French, Italian, and English. Featuring both local authors sharing their stories and international voices, this artsy spot also sells T-shirts, sunglasses, music, and unique creative gadgets, blending literature with lifestyle.

Libreria Anticuaria
Rafael Solaz

Carrer de Sant Ferran
7, 46001 Ciutat Vella,
libreriarafaelsolaz.es

One of the most enchanting bookshops in Valencia is housed in a historic building dating back to 1840. With over 15,000 books, Librería Anticuaria Rafael Solaz exudes a magical atmosphere reminiscent of the 'cemetery of forgotten books' from Carlos Ruiz Zafón's novel *The Shadow of the Wind*. Specialising in rare, antique, and curious books, the shop also offers vintage paper, engravings, postcards, and photographs.

Librería Bangarang

Carrer de l'Historiador Diago 9, 46007 Extramurs, insta @bangarang.vlc

The Librería Bangarang for comics and books is one of a kind. Besides selling books, they offer a space for like-minded individuals to gather for readings and workshops. One of their most popular events is Cuaderno Blablabla, where arts and literature come together.

Librería Ramon Llull

Carrer de la Corona 5, 46003 Ciutat Vella, llibreriaramonllull.com

The popular space Librería Ramon Llull hosts several book clubs, organises weekly readings, and hosts annual literature-themed costume parties. The shop offers its own curated book recommendations and features a dedicated children's corner to introduce young readers to the joys of books and storytelling.

Llibreries París

Carrer de Pelai 7, 46007 Extramurs, parisvalencia.com

Established in 1920, Llibreries París have long been a hub for book lovers in the city, offering a wide range of titles in various genres, including literature, history, philosophy, and art. Their four bookshops are especially recognised for their commitment to promoting both classic and contemporary authors.

Librería Regolf

Carrer del Mar 47, 46003 Ciutat Vella, llibreriaregolf.com

If you're looking for beautifully crafted maps of Valencia or Spain, Librería Regolf is the place to visit. Focusing on topographic maps, travel and mountain guides, and cartography, this bookshop is also the go-to destination for books on the region's flora and fauna.

Book Lovers Valencia

Carrer de Sevilla 5,
46006 L'Eixample,
bookloversvalencia.com

The only entirely English bookshop stocks over 12,000 new and second-hand books. They host events such as The Silent Book Club, Booklovers Unplugged, and meet-and-greets with international authors.

Librería Bartleby

Carrer de Cadis 50,
46006 L'Eixample,
libreriabartleby.com

Named after the character from Herman Melville's *Bartleby, the Scrivener*, Librería Bartleby embodies the spirit of curiosity, exploration, and a quiet love for reading, with a focus on contemporary fiction, Spanish and Latin American authors, and philosophy.

Re-Read Librería Lowcost

re-read.com

All second-hand books are priced at €4 each, €6 for two, and €12 for five at Re-Read Librería Lowcost. They also track the number of trees saved by giving these books a second life, promoting sustainability alongside great deals.

Ubik Café

Carrer del Literat Azorín 13, 46003 L'Eixample, insta @ubik_cafe

Ubik Café is a multi-disciplinary hub, serving as a restaurant, bar, library, bookshop, art gallery, and venue for concerts, dance, workshops, and readings. If you love being surrounded by books, you'll feel the unique magic of this place. Try the restaurant's *menu del día* for €13.

Librería la Batisfera

Carrer de Carles Ros 32, 46011 Poblats Maritims, insta @labatisferalibros

With a name inspired by Jules Verne's *Twenty Thousand Leagues Under the Sea*, Librería la Batisfera ('the bathysphere') evokes a sense of adventure and exploration. The bookshop offers a wide range of literary genres. There is also a bar name that hosts many cultural events.

El Asilo del Libro

Carrer de Sant Ferran 14, 46001 Ciutat Vella, insta @asilo_del_libro

The charming shop El Asilo del Libro offers an extensive collection of pre-loved books, including literary classics, history, art, philosophy, and fiction. It is a haven for bibliophiles, and anyone seeking out special or hard-to-find titles.

La Guarida de las Maravillas

Carrer de la Tapineria 12, 46001 Ciutat Vella, guaridadelasmaravillas.com

Librería La Guarida de las Maravillas is a place where readers can immerse themselves in a world of literary wonders, *maravillas*, offering a wide range of second-hand books. The shop's selection includes special and limited editions, making it an excellent destination for collectors.

ART SUPPLIES

Tapinearte
Bellas Artes

Carrer dels Assaonadors 13, 46001 Ciutat Vella, tapinearte.es

If you're an artist or a craft enthusiast visiting Valencia, Tapinearte Bellas Artes is worth checking out for all your creative supply needs! The shop supports the local art scene by providing artists with the tools they need and offering a space that celebrates creativity.

R. Vidal

Carrer de lu Blanqueria 8, 46003 Ciutat Vella, rvidal.es

R. Vidal is an established name in Valencia's art scene and has been serving the local artistic community for decades. Every artist knows this fully packed shop with quality supplies next to the Torres de Serranos.

Totenart

Carrer de la Corona 35b, 46003 Ciutat Vella, totenart.com

This shop hosts workshops, exhibitions, and art events to actively engage and support the local art community. Totenart offers a wide range of art supplies for any creative project, including painting materials, drawing tools, printmaking equipment, crafting supplies, canvases, papers, sculpture tools, and calligraphy essentials.

Batallón Manualidades

Carrer de Russafa 39, 46006 L'Eixample, batallon.es

This craft and hobby shop has everything you need for your creative projects. Whether you're looking for materials for scrapbooking, sewing, paper crafts, jewellery making, painting, home decor, or party supplies, Batallón Manualidades is the place to go.

Arte 43

Carrer del Literat Azorín 43, 46006 L'Eixample, arte43.es

The contemporary art gallery and shop Arte 43 is a unique spot in Valencia. The gallery regularly hosts exhibitions, art openings, and cultural events that contribute to the vibrant art scene in Ruzafa. Besides that, it is also a shop for art supplies.

Kowalski Bellas Artes

Carrer de Dénia 20, 46006 L'Eixample, kowalskicosasbellasartes.com

This shop offers much more than just art supplies. Kowalski Bellas Artes is a space that showcases and sells culture in many forms: music, literature, paintings, fashion, as well as unique objects and antiques. It's a place that truly inspires creativity for your own projects.

↓ LA POSTALERA (SEE PAGE 165)

↓ MERCAT DE TAPINERIA (SEE PAGE 154)

MADE IN VALENCIA

Alessandra Cola Art Studio & Gallery

Carrer de Calatrava 9, 46001 Ciutat Vella, insta @alessandracolaart

Alessandra, the artist behind Alessandra Cola Art Studio & Gallery, was born in Rome. Her art is deeply inspired by poetry as well as her frequent travels between Costa Rica and Valencia. Her work features vibrant colours, striking figures, and cheerful animals and suns with radiant smiles, creating warmth and joy.

El Podenco Arts & Crafts

Carrer del Museu 6, 46003 Ciutat Vella, insta @elpodencoartscrafts

The original art pieces of El Podenco Arts & Crafts are great gifts for any occasion. The pottery, one-of-a-kind bags, paintings, glass vases, jewellery, and clothes are all handmade.

Caos Community

Carrer del Museu 5, 46003 Ciutat Vella, caoscommunity.com

This art gallery showcases the work of urban artists, transforming them into limited edition items such as clothes, paintings, and sculptures. Using eco-friendly materials and a unique, full-ink printing method, Caos Community promotes both art and sustainability.

Sabotage Gallery

Carrer de la Puríssima 5, 46001 Ciutat Vella, insta @sabotagegallery

Sabotage Gallery serves as a hub for contemporary art and street culture, with a focus on urban art, graffiti, illustration, and other modern art forms. The raw, industrial aesthetic of Sabotage gives it a distinctive atmosphere, setting it apart from more traditional galleries.

Musgo Bazar

Carrer de Buenos Aires 5, 46004 L'Eixample, musgobazar.com

Whether you're looking for upcycled furniture, shopping for handmade accessories, or simply want to experience a bohemian atmosphere, Musgo Bazar offers something truly special. The shop's unique mix of vintage goods, local art, and eco-conscious products makes it a standout shop in the city's creative scene.

La Postalera

Carrer de les Danses 3, Carerr de la Corretgeria 4, 46001 Ciutat Vella, lapostalera.es

Looking for a unique souvenir from a local artist? You'll fall in love with the vibrant, colourful artworks inspired by Valencia and Mediterranean life. Choose from a variety of items including bags, badges and pins, ceramics, aprons, kitchen towels, cards, and posters.

Simple

Carrer del Palau 5, 46003 Ciutat Vella, simple.com

Everything in this shop is chosen with intention, creating a cohesive collection of items that are both practical and aesthetically pleasing. Simple sells Spanish products that are made to last, and the shop focuses on eco-friendly, sustainable production practices.

Atypical

Carrer dels Cavallers 10, 46001 Ciutat Vella, atypicalvalencia.com

Posters, calendars, T-shirts, postcards and magnets, all with a unique design celebrating the beautiful cuisine, culture, architecture, and nature of Valencia. The vibrant shop Atypical is showcasing the work of talented local artists.

VINYL & CDs

Digital records

Carrer de Castelló 5, 46004
L'Eixample,
digitalrecords.online

With its wide selection of new and second-hand records, particularly in electronic and indie genres, Digital Records offers a great mix of classic and contemporary music. The shop's involvement in the local music scene, its passionate staff, and its unique events make it a cultural hub for anyone interested in music.

Kultural Grooves

Carrer del Baró de San Petrillo 36, 46020 Benimaclet, kulturalgrooves.com

The extensive collection of soul, funk, jazz, electronic, and hip-hop vinyl at Kultural Grooves is a treasure trove for collectors and music lovers. Whether you're a DJ searching for rare finds, a casual listener looking for something new, or keen to discover Valencia's music scene, Kultural Grooves offers something for everyone.

Ultrasound Music

*Carrer de Cuba 49, 46006 L'Eixample, insta @ ultrasoundmusic_*

The record and music shop Ultrasound Music caters primarily to electronic music lovers, DJs, and collectors. The shop has earned a reputation as one of the go-to spots in the city for vinyl, DJ equipment, and other music-related gear, with a focus on genres like techno, house, electro, and ambient. It is a favourite among fans of local and international underground electronic music.

Discos Oldies

Carrer de la Mare de Déu de Gràcia 6, 46001 Ciutat Vella, insta @ discosoldiesvalencia

Known for its impressive collection of vintage music, Discos Oldies attracts collectors, music enthusiasts, and anyone with a love for vintage sound. With a focus on classic rock, pop, soul, jazz, and disco, customers can find records from iconic artists. Think of The Beatles, Led Zeppelin, The Rolling Stones, Elvis Presley, Marvin Gaye, and Aretha Franklin.

SHOPS WE LOVE

Espanista

Carrer de la Reina Na Maria 9, 46006 L'Eixample; Carrer dels Cavallers 8, 46001 Ciutat Vella, theespanista.com

Founded by Daniel Martínez after spending years abroad, Espanista blends community and creativity. They stock local and national products from small, innovative producers. Their customisable gift boxes, containing wine, art prints, and gourmet treats are most popular.

Alvent

Carrer de Calatrava 4, 46001 Ciutat Vella, alvent.com

Alvent is a jewellery brand with two boutiques in Valencia. It offers trendy and affordable jewellery, including earrings, necklaces, rings, piercings, and bracelets. The shop has excellent customer service, including free repairs and adjustments.

Turrones Ramos

Carrer de la Sombrereria 11, 46001 Ciutat Vella, turrones-ramos.es

With over 125 years of history, Turrones Ramos crafts its products in Jijona, using high-quality natural ingredients. They are known for their artisanal production of traditional Spanish sweets, especially *turrón*. Choose from classic varieties such as *turrón de nieve* (resembling marzipan), *turrón duro* (hard nougat), *turrón blando* (soft nougat), and *turrón de yema tostada* (topped with egg yolk and caramelised sugar).

Abanicos Vibenca

Plaça de Lope de Vega 5, 46001 Ciutat Vella, abanicosvibenca.es

Established in 1910, Abanicos Vibenca spans three generations of hand fan artisans in Valencia. Founded by Antonio Benlloch Martínez, whose unique painting style gained acclaim, it later evolved under his son Vicente Benlloch Palau. Today, grandson Vicente Benlloch Caballer carries on the family legacy, crafting and painting fans with traditional techniques.

Gnomo

Carrer de Dalt 24, 46003 Ciutat Vella, Carrer de Cuba 32, 46006 L'Eixample, gnomo.eu

The vibrant shop Gnomo offers design-focused gifts, home goods, and lifestyle products. Founded by Lucía Zarzuela and Gabriel Martínez, it features 1980s-inspired decor by Masquespacio. They are known for their commitment to personalised service and sustainability. Gnomo organises creative events and thoughtful campaigns, celebrating over a decade of innovation.

Pucherito Verde

Plaça del Miracle del Mocadoret 14, 46001 Ciutat Vella, insta @ pucherito_verde_handmade

Pucherito Verde is a boutique offering handmade, sustainable, and locally crafted goods. It features items like handcrafted jewellery, eco-conscious bags, and artistic accessories. The shop showcases products from Valencian designers, highlighting creativity, quality, and local craftsmanship.

Original CV

Plaça del Mercat 35, 46001 Ciutat Vella, originalcv.es

Isabel Reig founded Original CV in 2010. Her shop offers a curated selection of artisanal products such as wines, vermouth, oils, and sweets. The shop's mission is to bring the authentic flavours of the community to its customers, with items like gin flavoured with oranges from Valencia and black truffle oil.

PARKS AND SWIMMING

Parque de Cabecera

Parque de Cabecera is a tranquil urban park marking the start of the Jardín del Turia. It features a scenic artificial lake with rental boats shaped like swans and ducks in various colours. You'll find diverse Mediterranean vegetation, walking and cycling paths, and elevated viewpoints. Ideal for families and leisure, the park includes playgrounds, picnic areas, and a good connection to the nearby zoo, Bioparc. The 168,000-square-metre park was established in 2004. You can spot fish, turtles, and many bird species that call the park their home.

Jardines de Monforte

Very close to the city centre, you'll find a charming Neoclassical garden behind brick walls. Jardines de Monforte is known for its exquisite design and tranquillity. Spanning around 12,000 square metres, it features manicured hedges, ornate fountains, classical sculptures, and romantic pathways. The labyrinth layouts, shaded alcoves, and serene central pond are some of its main features. Once a private 19th-century estate, it is now a peaceful retreat for visitors. Its intimate atmosphere and historical charm make it a favourite for strolls, (wedding) photography, and moments of quiet reflection.

Jardines Real

The Jardines del Real are also known as Viveros Gardens. It is a historic park renowned for its expansive green spaces and cultural significance. Once home

to a royal palace, it now features lush gardens, ornate fountains, and diverse flora. Some highlights are the aviary with tropical birds, the rose garden, the children's playground traffic park, sculptures, shaded pathways, and areas for leisure and sports. The garden hosts cultural events like the summer festival concerts and houses the Valencia History Museum. It is a perfect blend of history, nature, and recreation.

Jardín del Turía

The Jardín del Turía stretches nearly 10 kilometres through the city. Created on the former Turia riverbed, it became one of Europe's largest urban parks after the river was diverted following catastrophic flooding in 1957. Divided into unique sections by seventeen bridges, it features lush gardens, sports facilities, playgrounds, fountains, and trails for walking, running, and cycling. Iconic landmarks along its path include the City of Arts and Sciences, Gulliver Park, and Bioparc Valencia. A green lung for the city, Jardín del Turía is a haven for recreation, culture, and relaxation.

Parque Central

Valencia's newest urban park was established in 2018. The modern park spans 110,000 square metres near the city centre and Ruzafa neighbourhood. Parque Central features themed gardens like La Vega de los Naranjos, which celebrates the city's orange grove heritage. Prominent water elements, including fountains and streams, enhance its beauty and ecological value. The park offers spaces for family activities, sports, and cultural events. Still expanding, it aims to connect neighbourhoods previously divided by railway tracks.

Playa de la Malvarrosa

Valencia's most famous beach is two kilometres long and in some parts 200 metres wide. Many students come to Playa de la

↓ JARDINES DE MONFORTE

Malvarrosa to relax between classes, or to play a game of beach volleyball on one of the many fields with some friends. It is not only busy during the summer months, but it is a perfect place to meet others, sunbathe, have some lunch or take a long beach walk all year around. There are wheelchair paths and both toilets and showers that are accessible.

Parque del Oeste

Parque del Oeste is a recreational area that opened in 1995, covering 43,750 square metres. The park was developed on the site of former Air Force barracks. The park features family-friendly spaces, including a children's playground, a skating rink, a mini golf course, table tennis tables, two basketball courts, and even an outdoor venue for concerts and events. The park is home to a variety of native plants, such as palm trees, oaks, and poplars. From June to September, the Olympic-size outdoor swimming pool is open to visitors.

Playa Patacona

Located in Alboraya, just north of Valencia, Playa Patacona is a tranquil beach. It is known for its golden sand and clear waters. It offers a family-friendly atmosphere with calm seas and is ideal for swimming as well as sunbathing. The beach has a promenade lined with lovely bars and restaurants, perfect for enjoying meals with a sea view. With beach sports, walking paths, and good amenities, including showers and sunbeds, Playa Patacona is a relaxing and accessible beach area.

VEGETARIAN AND VEGAN VALENCIA

FOOD

Mestiza

Carrer de la Reina 186, 46011 Poblats Maritims, insta @mestiza_cabanyal

The 1923 orange Cabañal building houses this plant-based restaurant. Try the beetroot tartare 'meatballs', jackfruit taco or the courgette spaghetti. The chefs at Mestiza are not afraid to use many different ingredients and flavours, and even hardened carnivores will enjoy dining here.

Copenhagen & Oslo

Carrer del Literat Azorín 8, 46006 L'Eixample; Carrer dels Catalans 8, 46001 Ciutat Vella, restaurantecopenhagen.es

Copenhagen & Oslo are vegetarian and vegan restaurants, known for their fresh, creative dishes and Scandinavian-inspired interiors. Copenhagen offers global flavours and affordable lunch menus. Oslo highlights local ingredients with a charming ambience.

Disidente Restaurante

Carrer del Comte de Salvatierra 41, 46004 L'Eixample, disidenterestaurante.com

Chef Juan Llorca, nutritionist Johnny Ondina, and football player Saúl Ñíguez lead Disidente Restaurante. Their vision focuses on creative, plant-forward dining, and 90% of their dishes are plant-based, yet all are indulgent and flavourful. They aim to break culinary norms while promoting healthy eating in an inviting, innovative space.

La Tastaolletes

Carrer de Salvador Giner 6, 46003 Ciutat Vella, latastaolletes.es

This vegetarian and vegan restaurant in Valencia's El Carmen district focuses on creative, healthy cuisine, highlighting *kilómetro cero* (local sourcing) and seasonal ingredients for sustainability. The diverse menu of La Tastaolletes includes delightful options like wraps, Buddha bowls, vegan lasagna, and desserts such as tiramisu.

Suc de Lluna

Carrer de Jorge Juan 19, 46004 Ensanche, insta @sucdelluna

On Mercado de Colón, you will find biocafé Suc de Lluna. It is run by agronomic engineers who are passionate about sustainability and ecological agriculture. They work with local products and advocate for active mobility, such as cycling. Known for their vegan-friendly, healthy meals, they combine social values with fresh, organic ingredients in a welcoming atmosphere.

Khambú

Carrer de Quart 41b, 46001 Ciutat Vella, khambu.com

Khambú's motto is 'Vegan food is good mood'. The owners are passionate about promoting sustainable, ethical eating through creative food made with fresh, locally sourced ingredients. A fast-food restaurant with excellent healthy and vegan food, this burger and sandwich place is popular with vegans as well as meat-eaters.

Almalibre Açai house

Carrer de Roteros 16, 46003 Ciutat Vella, almalibreacaihouse.com

This vibrant spot is known for its açai bowls and plant-based meals. At Almalibre Açaí House, the focus is on healthy, vegan, and vegetarian dishes made with fresh, organic ingredients. Situated on a charming street in El Carmen, the place has a relaxing vibe, perfect for enjoying a tasty, nutritious meal or getting some work done while sipping on a smoothie.

The Began

Carrer de Jaume Esteve Cubells 1, 46020 Benimaclet, insta @thebeganvalencia

As soon as you enter fast-food restaurant The Began, it is clear what they stand for. The walls boast slogans like *no meat, no plastic, no violence*; *vegan is not a diet, it's a lifestyle*; and *all you need are plants*. On the menu, you'll find Beganbab, Hot began, and Quesadillas with vegan cheddar.

Winebar Amberes

Carrer de Boix 4, 46003 Ciutat Vella, restauranteamberes.com

A wide range of organic wines, paired with plant-based and vegetarian dishes, like vegan tartar, croquettes, and cheese boards are served at Winebar Amberes. The clean and warm interior creates an inviting atmosphere. Amberes focuses on sustainable dining, blending traditional Valencian flavours with modern, eco-friendly practices.

Guakame Streetfood

Carrer del Mur de Santa Anna 3, 46003 Ciutat Vella, guakamestreetfood.com

For playful vegan dining, you should visit Guakame Streetfood. They offer dishes like BBQ-style cauliflower wings, creative burgers, and vegan desserts like chocolate-filled tacos with ice cream. The neon-lit interior channels a Tokyo-inspired aesthetic, creating a lively atmosphere enhanced by drag shows and DJ nights. Founders and influencers Jonan Wiergo and Christian Tomás aim to make vegan food appealing to all.

Kukla

Carrer de Palomino 8, 46003 Ciutat Vella, kuklavalencia.com

The owners Ayelet and Ronen brought their culinary roots from Tel Aviv to open the Middle Eastern restaurant Kukla. The vegan and vegetarian dishes they prepare are inspired by their grandmothers' cooking. Kukla is celebrated for dishes like *baba ganoush* and *fatoush salad*, and it focuses on fresh, authentic flavours.

Café Madrigal

Carrer de Puerto Rico 41, 46006 L'Eixample, cafemadrigal.es

The creative vegan dishes at Café Madrigal are made with love for food and for their customers. The menu features dishes such as vegan tortillas, gluten-free bread, and flavourful curries, cakes, and tasty salads, all made with quality ingredients. Guests can enjoy indoor or outdoor seating.

Let it Bloom

Carrer de Francesc Sempere 4, 46004 L'Eixample, insta @let_it_bloom_vlc

The vegan breakfast and brunch hotspot Let it Bloom opened in August 2024. They serve fresh, Mediterranean-inspired dishes with plant-based ingredients. Popular menu items include chickpea omelettes with spicy mustard cream and mushrooms, avocado toast with dukkah, rocket and radish, croquettes with quinoa, black olives, and almonds. The café also features specialty coffees.

La Casa Viva

Carrer de Cadis 76, 46006 L'Eixample, lacasaviva.com

La Casa Viva invites you to pause and enjoy the simple pleasures of life while savouring their delicious vegetarian and vegan dishes. Try the pizza, risotto, yucca fries, or vegetable lasagna, all made with fresh, plant-based ingredients that are as nourishing as they are flavourful.

Jardín Urbano

Carrer de Pere III el Gran 26, 46005 L'Eixample, jardinurbano.club

You might think Jardín Urbano is a library, a garden, a coworking space or an art gallery. It is all in one! Their menu includes a variety of plant-based dishes, such as burgers, sandwiches, and tapas. Jardín Urbano is popular for its dedication to eco-conscious dining, and it is a pleasant place to work and enjoy a moment alone or with friends.

Lo de Ponxe

Plaça de Rojas Clemente 5, 46008 Extramurs, insta @lodeponxe

Lo de Ponxe offers daily changing macrobiotic menus filled with a variety of grains, vegetables, and beans, creating vibrant, healthy vegan dishes. You might enjoy vine leaves with quinoa and sweet and sour sauce, paired with a red lentil cake, beetroot tartare, and avocado. If you're lucky, they'll serve their delightful papaya, lime, and almond custard with chia jam and coconut chips for dessert.

Les Maduixes

Carrer de Daoiz i Velarde 4, 46021 Algirós, restaurantemaduixes.es

Slow cooking is something Les Maduixes has practiced since 1986. A pioneering vegetarian restaurant it has been preparing everything slowly, artisanal, and creatively with the best local ingredients. Based on practices that respect the environment and healthy, home-made cooking, they have achieved the most authentic and unique flavours.

Artesano Vegano

Carrer de Martí Grajales 4, 46011 Poblats Marítims, insta @artesano_vegano_cristinavicent

On Valencia's Cabañal Market, you can find Artesano Vegano. They offer a variety of delicious vegan food, including homemade burgers, skewers, and pâtés. Cristina, the owner, transitioned from a traditional family business in poultry to a focus on vegan cuisine after her studies in nutrition and macrobiotics. Her stall features many plant-based options, such as the popular rice and chickpea burger, as well as items like hummus and vegan chorizo.

Herbolario Navarro

Carrer de Sant Vicent Màrtir 63, 46002 Ciutat Vella, insta @herbolarionavarro

Herbolario Navarro has been in business since 1771, selling herbal medicine, natural products, and eco-friendly wellness options. Their lunchroom offers a variety of plant-based dishes. The menu includes vegan cakes, sandwiches, and bowls, with many items made from organic ingredients. They also serve vegan-friendly breakfast options, like croissants, smoothies, and granola bowls. It's an excellent spot for a nutritious meal or snack while shopping for organic products.

NON-FOOD

Pangala slow bags and home

Carrer de na Jordana 2, 46003 Ciutat Vella, pangala.es

The boutique Pangala Slow Bags and Home stocks eco-friendly, handmade bags and home accessories. It offers a variety of products, including vegan leather bags, backpacks, and purses, designed with sustainability in mind. Located in the heart of the city, it aims to provide unique, sustainable fashion options for eco-aware shoppers.

Clotsy Brand

Carrer de Colón 72, 46004 L'Eixample, clotsybrand.com

The sustainable fashion label Clotsy Brand was established in Valencia in 2020 by Ángela Gómez and Alfonso Saura. The brand focuses on eco-friendly clothes made from organic and recycled materials. In 2022, they opened their first brick-and-mortar shop in Ruzafa, raising money via crowdfunding, highlighting their commitment to the community and ethical fashion.

The Blossomcare Company

Carrer de Martí 24, 46005 L'Eixample, theblossomcare.com

The Blossomcare Company specialises in vegan, niche perfumes. The shop offers a wide variety of products, including fragrances for personal use, home diffusers, and specialty items like pillow sprays and essential oils. Their range focuses on eco-conscious, cruelty-free options, emphasising high-quality ingredients.

OUTSIDE OF VALENCIA

Albufera

The freshwater lagoon and natural park Albufera, just ten kilometres away from the city, is known for biodiversity and tranquil beauty. Spanning over 21,000 hectares, you will find rice fields, wetlands, and a diverse wildlife, including rare bird species. You can enjoy boat rides or scenic walks, and savour traditional dishes like paella, which originated here. A haven for nature lovers, birdwatchers, and foodies.

Port Saplaya

Often referred to as 'Little Venice', Port Saplaya is a picturesque coastal destination ten kilometres north of Valencia. It is known for its charming canals, colourful buildings, and unique blend of seaside relaxation and vibrant local culture. Visitors can enjoy sandy beaches, waterfront promenades, and a variety of activities, including kayaking and boat trips. The area also has a wide selection of restaurants and cafés serving Mediterranean cuisine.

Xàtiva

Xàtiva is a historical town located sixty kilometres south of Valencia, famous for its stunning castle perched on top of the hill.

Divided into two parts (Castillo Mayor and Castillo Menor), it showcases a blend of Iberian, Roman, and Moorish architectural influences. It played a strategic role in ancient times and offers breathtaking views of the surrounding valleys. You at the castle via a scenic tourist train or on foot. The pleasant village has, numerous restaurants, and a rich history.

Requena

Take the ferry from Nagymaros

Requena is located seventy kilometres inland. This historic town is renowned for its well-preserved medieval architecture and wine culture. Its old town, Barrio de la Villa, has narrow streets, ancient churches, and charming plazas. The area is famed for its bodegas (wineries), producing excellent wines,

↓ XÀTIVA

particularly the native Bobal variety. Many bodegas offer tours and tastings, blending tradition with modern winemaking techniques.

Sagunto

Sagunto, thirty kilometres north of Valencia, traces its history to Iberian times, later thriving under Roman rule. Its Roman Theatre, built in the 1st century CE, is a remarkable example of ancient engineering. Nestled on a hillside, it accommodated 6,000 spectators and featured excellent acoustics. Restored in the 20th century, it now hosts cultural events. The town's layered past, including its medieval castle and Jewish quarter, makes it a fascinating destination.

Buñol

This village is known for the annual La Tomatina festival. Forty kilometres inland, it is easy to reach by train. The Cueva del Turche waterfall is a serene spot, surrounded by vegetation and a natural pool, perfect for a relaxing escape. Buñol also offers excellent hiking trails, such as routes through the Sierra de Malacara, with panoramic views and varied terrains. Combining cultural richness and natural wonders, Buñol is a great destination for adventurers.

Montanejos

Ninety kilometres from Valencia in the Castellón province, lies Montanejos, a haven for nature lovers. Renowned for its thermal hot springs, which maintain a water temperature of 25 degrees all year, the Mijares River offers mineral-rich waters surrounded by dramatic cliffs. Hiking enthusiasts can explore trails like the Sendero de los Estrechos, for breathtaking river gorges and mountainous landscapes. The rugged Sierra de Espadán mountains provide astonishing views and a diverse wildlife.

Riba-roja de Túria

At thirty kilometres from Valencia, you'll find Riba-roja de Túria. Its origins trace back to Iberian and Roman settlements, with a medieval castle symbolising its strategic importance during the Moorish and Christian eras. The town is deeply connected to the River Turia, offering the Parque Fluvial del Turia for swimming in summer, hiking, cycling, and picnicking along the lush banks. Recreational areas like Les Rodanes offer diverse landscapes, making Riba-roja a wonderful mix of history, nature, and leisure.

Navajas

The village of Navajas in the Castellón province sixty kilometres from Valencia, is renowned for the Salto de la Novia waterfall, a stunning sixty-metre cascade. The legend of the Salto de la Novia tells of a bride who leapt into the waterfall's depths in despair after her groom drowned during a ritual leap across the river, symbolising eternal love. Surrounded by lush nature, the refreshing pools are a perfect spot for swimming and enjoying beautiful landscapes. The area offers hiking trails in pine forests and historical sites.

INDEX

Districts 8
Travel 14
Where to stay 18
Good to know 22
When to travel 28
History 40
Sightseeing 48
Street art 62
Cinema 66
Festivals 70
Things to do 74
Famous people 80
Films & series in and about Valencia 84
Books in & about Valencia 88
Fun facts 94
Photo spots 98
Food and drinks 104
Going out 126
Shopping 140
Green Valencia 170
Outside of Valencia 184

FOOD AND DRINKS 104
Breakfast, brunch & coffee 106
Bluebell Coffee Co. 108
Boscon Coffee 108
Brunch Corner 108
Café ArtySana 106
DDL Boutique 106
Eggcellent 107
Eras Pan Tienda 106
Federal Café 107
Horchatería Santa Catalina 108
Mas Bonita, La 106
Nuez Café 107
Petite Brioche, La 107
Bring the parents 125
Bouet 125
Dos Estaciones 125
Vaqueta Gastro Mercat

Dinner 115
Begin 121
Damura Ramen 119
Diva, La 120
Estación Cero 121
Éter 120
Finestra, La 117
Hundred Burgers 122
Latte & Farina 119
Madre 122
Mamma Pazzo 119
Maui Fussafa 117
Ofrenda, La 121
Saona 117
Somos Raro Restaurante 117
Tinto Fino Ultramarino 115
Voltereta Bali 122
Zazu 121
Food markets 114
Mercabañal 114
Mercader 115
Mercado de Colón 115
Mercado de la Imprenta 114
Paella & other rice dishes 109
Bar Cremaet, El 109
Restaurante Navarro 109
Restaurante Panorama 109
Tasqueta del Mercat, La 109
Tapas & street food 110
100 Montaditos 110
Bar Cabanyal 114
Bodega la Peseta 112
Bodega La Rentaora 111
Chata Ultramarinos, La 112
Malvón 110
Pizzeria Raices 112
Quesometero Cheesebar 111
Sagardi 112
Taberna La Sénia 114
Tanto Monta 110

GOING OUT 126
Clubs 137
Akuarela Platja 137
Club Mya & Umbracle 137
Discoteca Indiana 138
Fox Congo 137
La3 138
Marina Beach Club 137
Mini Club 138
Play Club 138
Rumbo 144 139
Cocktail bars & rooftops 128
Apotheke 129
Atenea Sky 128
Café de las Horas 129
Café de Madrid 128
Gran Martínez 128
Jungle, The 128
Maison Lupin 130
Palacio Santa Clara 129
Live Music 133
Artist Bar, The 133
Black Note Club 134
Café del Duende 135
Fabrica de Hielo 133
Jimmy Glass Jazz Bar 134
Loco Club 134
Matisse Club 135
Peter Rock Club 135
Radio City 134
Vitti, La 135
Pubs & wine bars 131
Boba y el Gato Rnacio, La 133
Bodega Filià El Labrador 131
Café Berlin 131
Café Negrito 131
Cuatro Monos 132
Parabarap 132
St. Patrick's 132
Vive Vino Natural Wine Bar 132
Queer 139
Barberbirborbur 139
Deseo 54 139
Muse, The 139

MUSEUMS 54
Àgora – CaixaForum 57
Almoina, l' 58
Étno, l' 56
Fallas Museum 57
Fundación Bancaja 58
Hortensia Herrero Art Centre 55
IVAM 54
Museo Ciencias Naturales 56
Museo de la Seda 58
Museo del Patriarca 59
Museo Histórico de Valencia 57
Museo Mundo de Illusiones 56
MuVIM 54
Palacio del Marqués de dos Aguas 59
Science Museum 54

PHOTO SPOTS 98
Botanic Garden, The 102
Cabañal, El 101
Malvarrosa beach 101
Marina Real Juan Carlos I 102
Miguelete tower, El 98
Museo de Bellas Artes 101
Palau les Arts 102
Puente de las Flores 98
Umbracle, l' 98

SHOPPING 140
Art supplies 162
Bookshops 158
Asilo del Libro, El 161
Book Lovers Valencia 160
Doctor Sax, El 158
Guardia de las Maravillas, La 161
Libreria Anticuaria 158
Libreria Bangarang 159
Libreria Bartleby 160
Libreria la Batisfera 161
Libreria Patagoina 158
Libreria Ramon Llull 159
Libreria Regolf 159
Libreries Paris 159
Re-Read Libreria Lowcost 160

Ubik Café 161
Department stores 154
Flea markets, vintage & second-hand 144
3 Coolcats Vintage & Retro 149
Aleclé Vintage 147
Chase Retro & Med, La 149
Flamingos Vintage Kilo 144
Koopera Store 147
LAKA 149
Lavespa Roja 146
Mon Petit Secret 148
Monstruo, El 146
Rastro, El 144
Reborn Vintage Atelier 147
Reused.es 148
SoHo del Carmren 146
Street markets 144
Vintaker 148
How to dress like a local 142
Made in Valencia 164
Shops we love 168
Streetwear 152
Gondwana Surf 153
GOT'EM VLC 153
Grimey Store 152
Kaotiko 153
Legit Sneaker House 153
Nude Project 152
PSTR Store 152
Skateworld SW Best Brands 152
Studio Store VLC 152
Vinyl & CDs 166
Digital records 166
Discos Oldies 167
Kultural Grooves 167
Ultrasound Music 167

SIGHTSEEING 48
Ayuntamienot 50
Basilica de Mare de Déu 48
Cathedral of Santa Maria 51
Centro del Carmen 52
City of Arts and Sciences 49
Estación del Norte 49
Mercado Colón 52
Torres de Serranos 48
Veles e Vents 50
Water Tribunal of Valencia 53

VEGETARIAN & VEGAN VALENCIA 177
Almalibre Açai House 178
Artesano Vegano 181
Began, The 179
Blossomcare Company, The 183
Café Madrigal 180
Casa Viva, la 180
Clotsy Brand 182
Copenhagen & Oslo 177
Disidente Restaurante 177
Guakame Streetfood 179
Herbolario Navarro 182
Jardin Urbano 181
Khambú 178
Kukla 180
Let it Bloom 180
Lo de Ponxe 181
Maduixes, Les 181
Mestiza 177
Pangala slow bags and home 182
Suc de Lluna 178
Tastaollettes, La 178
Winebar Amberes 179

WHERE TO STAY 18
Cantagua Youth Hostel 21
Capsule Inn 18
Casual Valencia Vintage 19
Home Youth Hostel Valencia 18
Mythic Valencia 19
Nap V 19
Red & Purple Nest Hostel 18
River Hostel, The 18
Up Hostel 19
DWO Hostels 21
Bird House 21
Urban Youth Hostel 21

ABOUT THE AUTHOR

Fleur van de Put

Fleur is a Valencia-based writer, storyteller, and cultural enthusiast with a deep connection to the city. Originally from the Netherlands, she has embraced Valencia as her home since 2008, immersing herself in its rich history, dynamic culture, and Mediterranean lifestyle. Fluent in multiple languages, including English, she bridges the gap between locals and visitors, offering insightful perspectives on the city's landmarks, traditions, and hidden treasures. Fleur's passion for Valencia shines through her work, whether she's uncovering lesser-known neighbourhoods, delving into historical narratives, or exploring its gastronomic delights. Her vibrant personality and expertise make her a trusted source for insights on Valencia. She works in tourism, writing for magazines, travel guides, and online platforms, as well as planning tailor-made trips and guiding groups.

WHY SHOULD I GO TO VALENCIA

the city you definitely need to visit before you turn 30 (or 130)

Published in 2025 by
mo'media Rotterdam,
The Netherlands, momedia.nl

Concept
mo'media

Text and address selection
Fleur van de Put

Art direction and illustration design
Jelle F. Post

Editing
Ezra van Wilgenburg, Maaike van Steekelenburg, special thanks to Iris Brans

Photography
David in den Bosch, Vincent van den Hoogen, Fleur van de Put, Visit Valencia, Agata Kadar, dietwalther, Melinda Nagy, Nikolai Sorokin, Alan Smithers, SerFF79 and others

WHY SHOULD I GO TO?
Information on all our travel guides on **WHYSHOULDIGOTO.COM**

All rights reserved. No part of this publication may be copied, displayed, extracted, reproduced, utilised, stored in a retrieval system or transmitted in any form or by any means, electronic, mechanical or otherwise including but not limited to photocopying, recording, or scanning without the prior written permission of the publisher.

 Copyright © mo'media BV, 2025

Why Should I Go To Valencia
ISBN 978 94 9333 871 5
NUR 510

Disclaimer
The points of interested mentioned in this travel guide have been selected by the author. None of them have been paid for inclusion in this book: the *Why Should I Go To* book series is entirely ad-free.

Publisher's Note
Every effort has been made to ensure that the information in this book is accurate at the time of going to press. The publisher welcomes any information or suggestions for correction or improvement. Please send us an e-mail at info@momedia.nl.

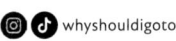 whyshouldigoto

Why Should I Go To travel guides are available for the following cities: Amsterdam, Antwerp, Barcelona, Berlin, Budapest, Copenhagen, London, Paris, Prague and Valencia. More cities will be added soon.